Home Maintenance

Complete DIY Guide

101 Ways to Look After
Your Home & Save Money

Ian Anderson MSc LCGI

HANDYCROWD MEDIA

Home Maintenance Checklist
Complete DIY Guide for Homeowners

101 Ways to Look After
Your Home & Save Money

Copyright © 2019 by Ian Anderson, who has asserted his right to be identified as the author of this work in accordance with the Copyright, Designs and Patents Act 1988.

All rights reserved. No part of this publication may be reproduced, stored in a retrieval system, or transmitted in any form or by any means electronic, mechanical, photocopying, recording or otherwise, without the prior permission of the copyright owner. But I'm pretty cool about that sort of thing, so for any enquiries regarding use please email Ian Anderson: ian@handycrowd.com

Published by handycrowd media Reg No. 995979268 Norway

ISBN 978-82-93249-10-8

Disclaimer: The author has made every effort to ensure that the information in this book is accurate. However, since it cannot be determined what you intend to do with this information or how competent you are, it shall be your own responsibility to ensure this information meets your specific requirements.

The author is a professional builder educated in the UK and the working practices and observations in this book reflect this. It is your responsibility to ensure the advice given in this book is suitable for your country or situation as working practices and rules differ from country to country. It is your responsibility as the homeowner to ensure you have permission to carry out alterations and additions to your home.

Seek local professional advice if you are in any way unsure.

I dedicate this book to my mother, Veronica Anderson who was the driving force behind the paintbrushes (as well as my father) in our house as we grew up.

CONTENTS

Preface	vii
Dull but Important Safety Notice	viii
Introduction	1
An Expensive Example	2
What Needs Maintaining?	3
Oh, But I Don't Know Anything About Maintenance!	5
The Five Absolute Basics of Maintenance	6
Cleaning	7
Regular Cleaning is More Effective (and easier)	8
Lubricants	11
Common Lubricants	13
Making Timely Adjustments	18
Loose Stuff	19
Stuff that's too Tight	21
Replacing Service Parts	22
Maintaining Different Materials	25
Proper Preparation Before Replacing Finishes	27
Timber Maintenance	29
Masonry Maintenance	31
Plaster Maintenance	36
Roof Maintenance	36
Pipe Maintenance	37
Metal Maintenance	40
Rust as a Finish	44
Plastic Maintenance	45
Rubber Maintenance	46
Fabric Maintenance	49
Maintenance Schedules	51
Unscheduled Maintenance	52
Vehicle Maintenance	53
Home Maintenance Checklist 101	56
Don't Put off the Inevitable	56
The Big Outdoors	58
Hard Standing Areas	58
Drains	59
Main Structure	63
Masonry/Walls/Brick/Block/Stone/ETC	63

Vegetation	67
Rendered and Painted Finishes	67
Doors and Windows	*68*
Roofline	*70*
Gutters and Downpipes	71
Fascia, Soffits, Verges and Barge Boards	71
Verges	72
Roof	*73*
Valleys	75
Chimney	76
TV Equipment	78
Indoors	**79**
Basements	*79*
Flooring	*80*
Walls	*81*
Ceilings	*82*
Windows	*82*
Doors	*84*
Kitchen and or Utility Areas	*85*
Cabinets/Doors	85
Kitchen Sink	86
Cooker Hood/Extract	87
Refrigerator	87
Washing Machine	89
Tumble Dryers (really, you're still using one?)	90
Bathroom	*91*
Damp	91
Silicone Sealant	91
Mould	93
Extract Fans	94
Plumbing	*94*
Taps and Faucets	94
Water Traps (in general)	95
Waste Pipes	96
Boilers/Heaters/Air Conditioning	97
Overflows	98
External Taps and Pipes.	98
Electrical system	*99*
Safety Trip Switch	99
Switches and Power Outlets	99

Appliances	100
Loft or Attic	*100*
Water Leaks	100
Insulation	101
Water Tanks	102
Ventilation	103
Fan Ducting	103
Unwanted Creatures	104
Epilogue	**109**
Getting in Touch	109
Contact Details	109
Companion Website	110
Subscribe	110
About the Author	**111**
Annual Maintenance Planning Notes	**112**
Additional Notes	**118**
Another Book by Ian...	**119**

PREFACE

Let's be honest here, home maintenance has a huge image problem. It's not cool, it's not sexy and it definitely isn't ever going to beat the thrill of building something new and shiny, not ever... But guess what; you know that new and shiny thing you're building instead of maintaining your home? Yup, it's going to need maintaining to keep that new and shiny look you so desire.

So relax a little, surrender to it, and since you can't truly escape it anyway, let a little maintenance creep into your life. Your stuff will love you for it and you'll get to fall in love with things all over again for looking so good, and oh; the planet will quite like you for it too.

Now I know I called this book a 'checklist' and if you're keen to get started right away you can jump straight to the checklist (the contents are next); But I hope you'll pause a moment and read on, because I want to give you more than just a big 'to-do' list. I want to share with you what I've learned about maintenance and how to do it properly.

So join me, and let's get your house, your cabin (lucky you!), your boat (double lucky you!), your vehicles (yes, even your bike) and all your other stuff working well and looking great again...

DULL BUT IMPORTANT SAFETY NOTICE

This book talks about using tools, working with electrical items, climbing on ladders, roofs, or scaffolding etc. It also talks about working with heavy or potentially dangerous materials and machines. Staying safe **must** be your **No.1 priority**. You should wear the right personal protection equipment for the job and get into the habit of working safely, *every time*.

Go online and seek the specific advice you need to stay safe during your planned project, the hse.gov.uk and osha.gov websites are good places to start. People are hurt every minute of every day, whether it is you or not, is your choice.

I don't want to hear you hurt yourself because you did something reckless or dumb, because then I'd feel bad and you don't want that. Always take your time, be careful and for goodness sake *use your common sense, because if it feels unsafe or dangerous... it probably is!*

So be careful, this stuff can hurt... a lot...

INTRODUCTION

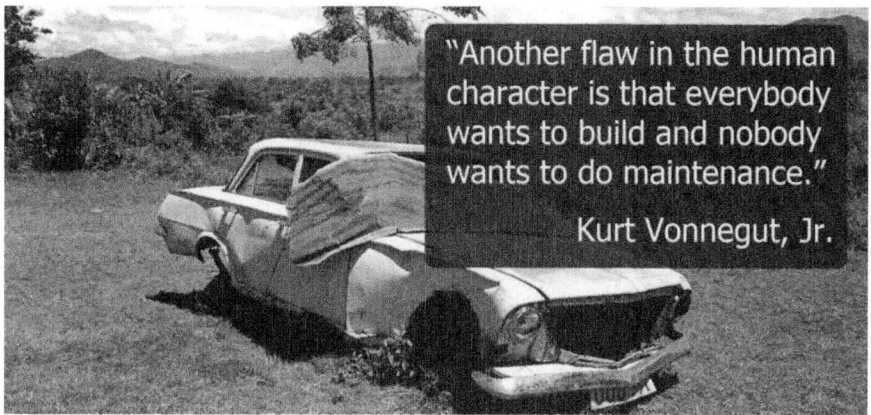

"Another flaw in the human character is that everybody wants to build and nobody wants to do maintenance."

Kurt Vonnegut, Jr.

I rather like the 'duffers' tool kit, which consists of a roll of tape and a can of WD40. The theory being; 'If something moves that shouldn't, you tape it up, and if something doesn't move, but should; you give it a squirt of WD40.'

Although intended as a joke; when it comes to maintenance it's actually pretty close to the truth, because a little goes a long way to keep your stuff looking good and performing well.

I understand some people think routine maintenance is a just a necessary 'evil', but routine maintenance (even if it's just to oil those squeaky hinges) will teach you lots of useful and practical things about stuff, including how to recognise when something's wrong.

The point of regular maintenance is to ensure your stuff functions as the manufacturer intended for the longest possible time and it's a fact that neglected stuff either wears out, breaks down, goes rotten or rusts away prematurely.

You've already invested your hard-earned money, so it makes perfect financial sense to spend a little more to keep it looking good and working well, thus protecting your original investment, as well as giving you years more use.

In addition, there's extra hassle if you don't maintain your stuff, because *Murphy's law* dictates it'll fail at some very inconvenient point. For example, your long-neglected lawnmower is more likely to cut out half way through cutting the lawn just before your big party than at any other time...

AN EXPENSIVE EXAMPLE

In case you need further convincing... As a contractor, I once billed a client close to £5000 ($6200) to repair a leaky gutter and wait, before you write me off as a 'rip off' builder, let me explain. The leaky gutter in question had been leaking for many decades with the guy who fitted it long dead. In fact, the gutter wasn't actually leaking as such, but rather so poorly positioned that the water simply ran down the wall instead. Fast forward to today and this fine old English farmhouse now had a big problem, well four actually...

- Spalled brickwork because the frost had frozen the saturated bricks and crumbled away their surface.
- A rotten timber window frame because the water had run onto and eventually inside the vulnerable timber.
- Several floor joist ends rotted away because they were sitting in a constantly damp wall (old solid walled cottage remember).
- The icing on the cake. The damp wood attracted some little beetles which made a nice, comfy home in the joists and floorboards, i.e. woodworm.

All were time consuming and messy jobs, especially replacing the ends of timber joists built into the wall, since part of the floor and ceilings needed removing for access. Oh, and don't forget the re-positioning of the original offending guttering as well...

I hope that true story illustrates how ignoring the maintenance on a house can get expensive. And you're going to have even bigger problems if you ignore the maintenance on anything with moving parts. Especially machines with parts operating at high speed that need lubrication (engines, gearboxes etc). When these things fail, they can be *catastrophic non-repairable failures*, i.e. terminal, dead, 'time to go shopping for a new one' kind of failure.

Sure sounds expensive to me.

WHAT NEEDS MAINTAINING?

Everything. Even so-called 'maintenance-free' stuff (an oxymoron if ever there was one) needs maintaining. Because time respects nothing, everything decays. But we can fight it, we can slow it down to an acceptable level. Just remember, the moment you stop fighting, time wins, every time.

Your secret weapon to fight the ravages of time is to pay regular attention to details. Because the details matter, they'll tell you what's going on with your stuff. So don't ignore them, notice the small changes on a day by day basis and act on them. Feel something loose? Tighten it. Notice the paints a bit dull on the window? Put it on the list of things to paint in the Easter break. Notice the waters going down the plughole slowly? Go get the plunger.

Don't ignore anything. Because the 'regular' part is the crucial thing about maintenance, because if you neglect it, you'll eventually need to repair failures and breakdowns. Remember, time *always* wins in the end

And here is the best part... maintenance is easy, quick, and it's cheap (a rare combination). But; repairs are more difficult, more complex, take much longer and use more materials. Oh, and the cost rockets upwards too. Plus, repairs are way more intrusive into your daily life, causing hassle I'm sure you don't need.

Take your door locks for example; you need to set aside some time once a year to maintain your locks. Wipe away any dirt or old lubricant (on a padlock for example, or if you've been brave enough to take the lock parts out of a door) and then add a little of the right lubricant into the keyway. It's that easy. Arguments abound on the best type of lubricant. But the truth is, any kind of lubricant is better than nothing, (arguments be damned!).

This simple and not terribly time-consuming maintenance job could make your locks last a lifetime. Most folks don't do it and then wonder why their locks are stiff, or their key breaks off in the lock, one dark, wet night when they come home late from the pub...

So, are we in agreement then? That to maintain your stuff is an absolute no-brainer? Yes? Brilliant!

introduction

OH, BUT I DON'T KNOW ANYTHING ABOUT MAINTENANCE!

You can learn more than you think just by looking at stuff. Because it doesn't matter whether you're maintaining a roof, any kind of vehicle (from a bike to a boat etc.) or a wardrobe; the basic principle is the same. You carry out maintenance to *preserve conditions* and *counter wear and tear*.

And everything needs some sort of maintenance, from the plastic window frames in your house to the chain on your bicycle. And as different as those two items are, so is the maintenance they need. One needs an occasional inspection for leaks and a wash to remove contaminants, and the other, a thorough degreasing and a squirt or three of oil every now and then. I'm sure you can tell which goes with which (don't worry, you soon will)...

The key to learning how to maintain something is to have a very basic understanding of how the components look and work. Don't panic, you don't need to know the science, just think about...

- How does it feel (the same as usual or different)?
- Is this supposed to move, (yes/no or is it stiff/loose)?
- Is that supposed to happen (catch/rub/wear/bang/clink/clonk etc.)?
- What vulnerable parts do I need to protect from corrosion or wear?
- What needs replacing regularly (service parts/paint/fluids/lubrication etc.)?

THE FIVE ABSOLUTE BASICS OF MAINTENANCE

The five elephants in the room let's say, all are obvious and yet so often ignored. Let's use the thoughts from the previous section to create a basic regime to keep your stuff looking good and working well. Use one or more of the following five basic preventative maintenance tasks, depending on what you're maintaining...

- Keep stuff clean (dirt, grit, dust, and tired or contaminated lube are bad).

- Lubricate vulnerable moving parts (lubricate and be free!)

- Make timely adjustments to stuff starting to wear. A few little tweaks can go a long way to stave off failure, (tighten a loose screw in a kitchen cupboard door hinge for example).

- Replace service parts on time (service parts are designed to wear out over time to protect delicate or more expensive parts).

- Maintain finish integrity (rust, rot & oxidisation are bad).

Ignoring any of the above leads to little problems, which over time turn into bigger problems and eventually, complete failures or breakdowns. For example, as we saw above in the leaky gutter example, if you fail to fix a leaky gutter, there's probably no immediate disastrous problem, but, in a few years, *you will* have additional damage to fix as well, guaranteed.

One more time: keep on top of small maintenance jobs when they are easy and cost little; the longer the interval between maintenance checks the larger the final bill for repairs.

Let's go over the five basic maintenance tasks in more detail...

CLEANING

I know, I know; you might think cleaning is repetitive and dull, but it *is* rewarding once you start. Cleaning away all that accumulated muck and revealing the gleaming surface underneath (especially on something you've rescued from the scrap heap) feels fantastic! You might even make it look brand new again. Not to mention the nice comments you'll get when people see it and comment 'Wow! That looks great!'

Keeping stuff clean from a maintenance standpoint isn't about making stuff look pretty (although it does); but rather more importantly, when you clean stuff, you remove the grit and other contaminants held in the build-up of muck (lubricants especially attract and hold dust and grit).

This gives your stuff a real reliability and longevity boost because tiny abrasive particles like grit increase friction, impede performance, and cause components, surfaces and finishes to wear out prematurely.

It's especially important to clean stuff before applying any new lubricants, otherwise you might push the aforementioned congealed contaminants and abrasives further into the working parts (not good).

Washing the car on Sunday for example, is not just to make it shiny; it serves a real practical purpose too. Because cleaning means getting up close and intimate with your stuff, you'll spot anything unusual or amiss very early on. You might notice a small, hardly visible malfunction; wear marks on a component or some tiny damage to a finish.

For example, after washing your car (and before polishing it, and yes you need to do this, in the spring and just before winter), you'll be able to fill any stone chips you found in the paintwork whilst washing it (see how in the *Metal Maintenance* section later).

Cleaning is also the first thing to do with 'new-to-you' used things coming into your home to help determine their true condition and to evaluate what repairs or improvements you need to do. At the very least, cleaning properly ensures it's fit to join your household by 'making it yours' and not harbouring any nasties, I mean, who wants other peoples 'dirt' in their home?

Don't underestimate the 'feel good' factor of cleaning either. For example, I like old cars and I love the look of newly polished paintwork. I think there's truth in the maxim "the older it is, the cleaner you keep it". I love to see clean windows and mirrors too (oh, or is that just me...?).

Remember how nice your home feels just before your mother in law comes to visit? (and don't you wish it could look like that all the time?!). Plus, you'll be less likely to throw things away, just because they're embarrassingly scruffy, (a win for the planet).

REGULAR CLEANING IS MORE EFFECTIVE (AND EASIER)

Regular gentle cleaning of things prevents excessive build-up of dirt and contaminants, so you never need to resort to more aggressive cleaning methods, which are hard work, take longer, risk causing damage, and cost more.

But if you've neglected your stuff, you might need to bring out the big guns like powerful chemicals. The upside is, you'll get mind bogglingly satisfying results from such deep cleaning because dirt and grime builds up unnoticeably slowly over time.

Plus, a deep clean might just re-reveal the once hidden beauty of the item in question. I've lost count of the times I've seen folks cleaning something up with the intention of selling it on, only to fall in love with it all over again. My mother used to complain bitterly that their cars were never so clean and shiny as the week before my father planned to sell them...

Build your cleaning into a routine (remember I polish my cars each spring and just before winter?). Nominate a time of week, month, or year etc., depending on what you're cleaning and stick to it.

After just one years use, this jigsaw needs cleaning to remove potentially damaging sawdust.

Pay particular attention to anything you own with vents or fans etc. because dust and shavings are naturally pulled into them, causing clogging and eventual overheating.

Once a year I clean all mine with a quick blast of compressed air. Use the tyre airline at the garage or buy a can of compressed air from an electronics shop if you don't have access to a small compressor. Aim through any vent slots or other openings, especially around any motors. In a pinch, a tickle with a paintbrush and a vacuum cleaner is better than nothing.

Remember that WD40 makes a mini high-pressure cleaner in certain situations too (not too close to electronics though). Use the thin tube on the WD40 can to blast out old lube, grit etc. (on a bicycle chain needing new lubrication for example), wipe off and then re-lubricate with the recommended lubricant (light machine oil for that bicycle chain).

Even if you are good and clean your stuff to a strict schedule, the following cleaning jobs need doing *on the spot* or as soon as you notice them...

- Wipe clean dirty outer casings, exteriors, and surfaces after use to prevent dirt becoming ingrained into the finish.
- Blow clear clogged ventilation grills and other cooling vents to keep them clean (prevents overheating).
- Clean away any gritty stuff (sand etc.) not only to prevent damage to finishes but also to prevent it contaminating any lube inside which leads to premature wear of mechanical components.
- Clean anything greasy before it gets the chance to attract the aforementioned grit and other contaminants (see above).
- Wash fabrics often. Dust and grot wears out fabrics prematurely, sweat is particularly corrosive (yuck!).

USING CHEMICALS

Hard work used to be the default method of cleaning, but today there are many different chemicals to do some of the 'scrubbing' for you. Bearing in mind the desired end result you want, study the *applications,* or *uses* on the packaging of the product to ensure it's suitable for your project (you can really damage stuff if you get this bit wrong). You can always double check with store staff if you need something, (especially symbols), explained in more detail. The store might also have additional technical sheets, especially related to using the product safely (many strong cleaning chemicals will burn skin and eyes).

Although the blurb on some packets might claim the product is a simple spray on and rinse off process, this is rarely the case and a good soak does wonders with nearly every cleaner, reducing 'elbow grease' dramatically. Spraying on a cleaner and then immediately attacking it with a brush wastes effort and chemical. Agitate the chemical well into the gunk with a brush for best penetration, repeating several times for even better results. Don't forget, old toothbrushes or paintbrushes are great for cleaning small or intricate stuff.

The exceptions to the above are the more powerful or acid-based cleaners, which *are* time sensitive. Reading the manufacturer's instructions is very important or they may remove more than you bargained for. Again, *always* protect your eyes and any exposed skin when using powerful cleaners.

LUBRICANTS

We can't talk about maintenance without talking about lubrication, a key component in keeping things going well. But lubricants do much more than you think, let's go through some of the wonderous benefits of lube...

- **Friction and wear**: If moving parts were to touch each other, friction would quickly wear them out. So we add a lubricant to keep moving components separate (it's a microscopic thing) and this prevents wear to individual parts by reducing or eliminating friction.

- **Self-lubricating parts**: Be aware that some components have special lubricating qualities and need no additional lubrication.

- **Sealed for life**: Some components contain all the lubrication they need to last the expected lifespan of the component. i.e. they are supposedly maintenance free. Problems arise if you want the item to last even longer, but the manufacturers would really rather you buy a new one...Check the manufacturer's information first.

- **Cooling**: Friction also builds heat as you know, and lubricants soak up this heat carrying it away from vulnerable components. The oil in an engine is a great example, it's not there just to lubricate, it acts as a coolant too.

- **Cleaning**: lubricant attracts and holds debris such as particles from the surroundings and the microscopic particles created by wear. This debris degrades the lubricants quality and is why lubricants need replacing from time to time. Engine oil turns from a golden honey colour to black goop for example.

  NOTE: Before replacing lubricant, first, you'll need to remove any existing lubrication (i.e. drain old engine oil or use a degreaser to remove old lube). Also, any lubricant filters (think engine oil filter), need replacing, thus removing any contaminants they contain.

- **Corrosion**: lubricants are great at preventing corrosion by excluding air and water and thus preventing the oxidising reaction.

- **Sealing**: lubricants help seal against air and water finding their way into places where they'd cause damage. Smearing petroleum jelly (Vaseline) onto a hosepipe O ring for example, not only helps facilitate repeated coupling and uncoupling, it will protect the seal making leaks less troublesome. Lubrication also helps seal gas or air tight fittings.

- **Power**: lubricants are incompressible, making them ideal to transfer power via hydraulic action. Telescopic rams on construction equipment or the fluid inside a vehicles automatic gear box for example.

In practice, lubricants can do other things too... You can free stuck or seized things with several soakings of a penetrating lubricant like WD40, which is a fish oil-based lubricant and water dispersal agent (although any penetrating type, thin oil should do the trick). Don't forget to give them plenty of time though. Some people even soak stuff like chains, cycle parts, padlocks, vehicle parts etc. in a lubricant (like diesel/ paraffin/ kerosene/ etc.) overnight to free everything up (wear gloves and ventilate though), before wiping off and adding a suitable, long term lubricant.

COMMON LUBRICANTS

Visually check any lubrication points or moving parts to identify what type of lubricant is already there (consult the original maintenance documents if possible or search online). Choose the same or similar specification (grade) lubricant for best results. Generally, slower moving things need thick lubricant like grease and faster moving things need thinner and high-performance lubricants (for their stickiness and stability under extreme conditions).

Be vigilant for any signs of stiffness, creaking or squeaking from any moving component, a sure sign the lubrication has dried out completely. Any seized component, (e.g. moving parts that don't) needs attention immediately or you risk other components breaking because of the extra stress the non-moving part adds. Here are a few of the most common lubricants...

WD40

WD-40 is the *40th* attempt to make a *Water Displacement* chemical and is very useful for lots of jobs. WD-40 has five basic properties:

- **Cleans**: WD-40 helps to dissolve dirt, grime, and grease. It also dissolves some adhesives, allowing removal of sticky labels etc.
- **Displaces Moisture**: WD-40 pushes out damp in some electrical systems helping to prevent moisture-related short circuits.
- **Penetrates**: WD-40 loosens rust-to-metal bonds and frees stuck, frozen, or rusted metal parts (or indeed any stuck parts).
- **Lubricates**: WD-40 is a light lubricant suitable for moving parts.
- **Protects**: WD-40 protects metal surfaces against rust with its corrosion-resistant ingredients.

LIGHT MACHINE OIL

Light machine oil is a thin, almost transparent oil, that has many uses around the home and garden, lubricating tools, hinges, nuts & bolts, firearms, bicycles, wheels, fans and sewing machines (remember the saying "runs like a sewing machine"? Light machine oil is responsible). It's highly refined and very thin, it gets into tiny spaces ensuring free movement. It's so thin you'll need a rag when using it; apply a few drops, work the mechanism and then wipe away any excess dripping down. Repeat as necessary. 3-in-one is one of the most famous brands.

ENGINE OIL

Engine oil is a heavier, often golden coloured lubricant available in many grades to suit different operating conditions. Although primarily for inside engines, engine oil makes a good all-round lubricant for many moving parts and is handy to have in the workshop in a little pump action oil can. Available in two broad types, organic or mineral and the more modern synthetic oils. Oil is measured by its viscosity when cold (w means winter) and when hot, hence the two numbers on the packaging e.g. 20w50. The 20 in this case wouldn't be very good for a cold engine in a cold climate, it's too thick and could impede starting and cold running. 5w40 would be better. The second number is the viscosity of the oil in a hot engine and needs to be higher to allow for the thinning that oil undergoes when heated.

However, used engine oil is a dangerous chemical cocktail and needs recycling safely, although some old timers swear by it painted onto rough metal stuff to stop corrosion. That may be useful if you own a tractor which lives in a field, but don't try it underneath a sports car which lives on your drive...

COPPER GREASE

Copper grease is a thick, very sticky, shiny copper coloured (unsurprisingly!) lubricant. Apply it to bolt threads when reassembling components as it prevents future corrosion and seizing (making future maintenance easier). Sometimes known as *anti-seize compound*. Also, commonly used sparingly on the back and edges of vehicle brake pad back plates to reduce squealing. Copper grease copes well with high temperatures and sticks well to moving parts.

GREASE (LITHIUM USUALLY)

Grease is a thick (often yellow looking) lubricant to protect against wear of moving parts on machines. Grease is very sticky (it's made from oil mixed with special soap) making it ideal for fast moving components like bearings, but also for slow moving components like, moving levers on machines, rotating parts, slides, and contact points like door latches etc. Apply grease directly to the parts, operate a few times to work it right in and wipe away any excess.

Grease Nipple (UK) or Zerk Fitting (USA)

Pump new grease into bearings via the spring loaded ball bearing at the tip

In addition, you might see grease nipples on some machines. Grease nipples (Zerk or Alemite fitting in the USA) allow you to easily push new grease directly into a bearing etc., using a special, (but cheap to buy), grease gun. Simply wipe the nipple and the nozzle on the gun clean, push the nozzle onto the grease nipple and pump (check the machines instructions for how many strokes) or until it oozes out of the bearing or vent hole.

DRY LUBRICANTS

Lots of smaller moving parts still need lubrication, but would be susceptible to gumming up over time, due to the accumulation of dust and debris sticking to wet lubricants. Things like lock cylinders for example. Your key needs to go in and out of a lock without getting all greasy every time. Enter dry lubricants. Old school (and still pretty good) is graphite (yup, the same stuff they make pencils out of) which is super slippery and ideal for inside dry mechanicals. Don't add graphite to anything previously greased though or you'll make a nasty black paste (thoroughly clean it with a degreaser or solvent and let it dry before switching to a dry lubricant).

Modern dry lubricants are a little more complicated than the stuff in pencils though. Look out for the word MOLY (short for Molybdenum disulfide). PTFE (short for polytetrafluorethylene) or for brand names like Teflon, a slippery material you'll already know about from non-stick pans.

There is one last dry lubricant (for humans!) that you might have forgotten about, a surprising one maybe, and that's talcum powder. As anyone who has ever danced on a floor dusted with the stuff or sprinkled it inside rubber trousers will attest. Oops, way too much info...

SPECIALIST LUBRICANT

You'll find all sorts of special lubricants in this bunch, maybe even one or two that you'd not thought of as lubricants...

- Silicone based lube for rubber seals, O rings, washers etc.
- High temperature lubricant for hot environments (it doesn't thin or run in high heat applications).
- Cold temperature lubricants for cold environments (it doesn't thicken and go stiff in conditions of extreme cold).
- Long life lubricant for difficult to access components or where you need a long service life.
- Food grade lubricants; designated safe to use on food processing machinery.
- Edible oils. Stops food sticking to surfaces during the cooking process itself, (think cooking oils etc.) as well as actually a foodstuff in itself (think olive oil etc.).
- Skin safe lubricants which don't harm sensitive skin or other areas; think lip balms, hand creams, sunscreen and other erm, let's just say... more intimate, personal lubricants, (I say old chap, steady on!).

DEGREASER

I'll add a note here about degreasers as you'll often need to use one before reapplying a lubricant. We use degreasers all the time in the home from washing the dishes to cleaning dead flies off car bumpers.

These light detergent-based degreasers are fine for general cleaning of lightly soiled surfaces or parts; but there are more industrial degreasers out there, designed to shift even the most stubborn grease or old lubricant. Often solvent based for spraying onto greasy surfaces or in liquid form for dipping smaller parts into. Follow the instructions carefully as some degreasers are more than powerful enough to damage surrounding finishes like paint.

Some of the solvents you have lying around (like petrol, alcohol, various spirits, lighter fluid etc.) are also brilliant for removing grease, but they are very flammable and dangerous. So you really shouldn't use them; but if you must (and I admit I sometimes do), at least ensure you have good ventilation and be careful not to spill any.

Be particularly careful how you dispose of any rags soaked in fuel etc., as they too are now flammable. Oh, and if you do screw up and burn your garage down, remember I did tell you not to use them, so don't come crying to me, I'll deny everything...

MAKING TIMELY ADJUSTMENTS

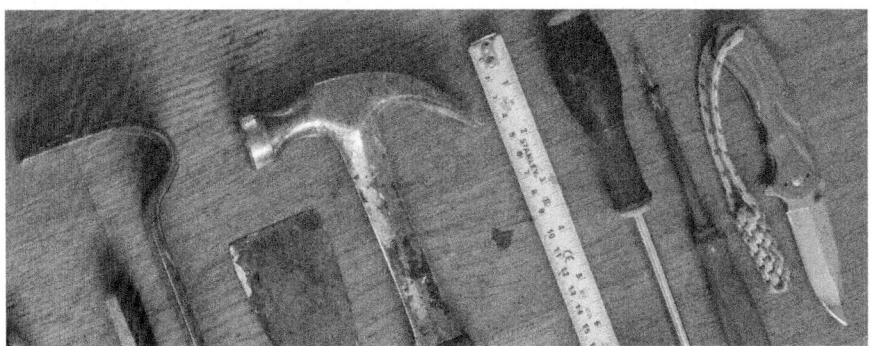

The song says, 'nothing stays the same' and this goes for most of the stuff in your life too. Little by little, friction wears away microscopic amounts of material. Eventually this causes stuff to require small adjustments to maintain a proper fit. Even if you properly maintain your stuff, moving parts will still wear down and although lubrication slows the process down considerably, eventually some adjustments are necessary to maintain ideal operation.

Usually you'll need to adjust something for one of two reasons; when something becomes either too loose or too tight. Sometimes this happens together; a loose cabinet hinge for example might make the door rub its neighbour. Unintentional physical contact nearly always causes excessive wear and tear on at least one of the parts affected.

Periodically, or better still, 'as-you-notice', examine moving parts closely and try to determine which parts should move freely, (like the hinge pin on a cabinet door for example) and what should be tight (like the screws holding the above hinge for example). Again, it only takes a few seconds to look at a cabinet hinge, turn the screw to pull the door back into line and it's fixed.

If you don't know how to adjust a cabinet hinge, experiment with the screws, move each one back and forth a little and look at the way the door moves, you'll soon figure out how each screw moves the door. Turn and check, turn and check! Often the screws which hold the hinge back plate into the cabinet itself loosen, allowing the door to drop or slop about, so check, adjust and tighten these first.

LOOSE STUFF

Anything that's loose causes wear in two ways. First, slack parts cause impact damage within themselves as they move around. A loose fastener for example moves around into opposite ends of its hole under load, causing the hole to become elongated. Over time, this movement compounds, further elongating or damaging the hole until one day the whole thing will tear out of the now much enlarged hole. For example, the screws holding up the handrail on your stairs will last indefinitely when they're tight. However, when loose they allow the handrail to move around, eventually tearing those screws right out of the wall. This damages and enlarges the holes, making it impossible to re-insert the screws. Second, loose fasteners or worn parts increase the range of movement of each part, often allowing parts to collide with other parts. Loose screws in a door hinge allows the door to hit the frame or worse, another door; bad news if it's a pair of glass doors on a bathroom cabinet or shower cubicle for example.

Checking bolts and other fixings for tightness periodically stops vibration shaking something completely loose (small engines such as those found on petrol lawnmowers are famous for this). In essence, trust your senses, i.e. look, feel, and listen for loose stuff as you go. Be aware enough to notice excess movement in your everyday stuff and either make a note of it for when you have more time or better still, adjust or tighten it on the spot, (get someone to buy you a Leatherman tool for Christmas...). It often only takes a few seconds to adjust or tighten a loose screw or fitting etc. for example, so don't ignore them!

However, be careful not to over tighten stuff, especially if it's something which repeatedly comes loose. If something repeatedly becomes loose, you really need to find out why. Look for vibration, catching or rubbing which might be causing stress on the fasteners or look at the way you use the item (i.e. are you abusing it!) Alternatively, if it's a nut and bolt type fastener, try adding a *shake proof washer* or try swapping the nut for a *shake-proof* one.

It's easier improve a fastener or to come back and give something an extra turn to nip it up than to fix a stripped thread. If you routinely over tighten fasteners and fixings, (making them difficult to undo), you're just building in difficulties to trip you up during future maintenance. Consider getting a torque wrench if you're going to play with nuts and bolts a lot (these wrenches apply a set amount of pressure, often published in the manual, thus removing the guess work).

STUFF THAT'S TOO TIGHT

Anything that's tight or a poor fit will suffer from vastly increasing friction and that might mean you need to use excessive force to operate the item. Repeatedly forcing something that's too tight can stress the whole construction, eventually leading to seizure or failure. Stuff that's catching or rubbing also wears out much faster.

Maintaining intended gaps between moving parts is vital for long life. Look, listen, and feel for catching parts, if something is tight or catching, find out why by examining closely how it works. Wear marks are often visible as rub marks in the finish. Try to determine if it needs lubrication, or if there is debris in the workings (e.g. dirt in tracks) or if fasteners or hardware have loosened or sagged, or even if there is extra material in the way, for example, wooden doors and/or frames often swell due to excess moisture.

For example, a door repeatedly pulled or even kicked to close or open it, will eventually become weak at its joints because of the stress caused by excessive twisting. This will eventually damage the frame too, removing paint or even loosening the frames fasteners. Fortunately, to tighten some screws, adjust a hinge, or plane a little off a door is not too difficult, just look at the gaps between the door and frame to find where it's tight and remove material where the paint shows wear marks until you have even gaps again. You want about the thickness of a coin all the way around.

Make sure any weather seals are not causing trouble as well (they are easy to dislodge) and don't forget to re-paint any bare surfaces.

Fix tight stuff by either cleaning, lubricating, tweaking adjusters, tightening fasteners, or removing excess material to increase clearance and ensure proper operation. Make sure the problem is not a symptom of another underlying problem though; you'll never manage to properly adjust a damaged cabinet hinge for example.

Going back to the door example, if an outside wooden door starts catching, is it swelling because damaged paint is letting rainwater get into it? Or water from a leaky gutter? Or because of poor drainage in front of the door? Or excessive splash back from 'too-high' ground levels? Or is it catching because of loose hinge fasteners? Or even loose frame fasteners? Wow, that's a lot of "or's"...

REPLACING SERVICE PARTS

Some things are simply not possible to maintain by simply looking after them, because they contain parts specifically designed to wear out (I know, you'd think that would be shocking huh, but wait...). It might seem a nuisance, but service items are there to protect the more expensive parts, thus actually *saving* you money, (see, so it's not all bad!).

Therefore, ignoring or failing to replace service parts makes no financial sense at all. An oil filter and fresh oil for example costs peanuts when compared to repairing an engine damaged by an ineffective oil filter clogged with contaminated old oil.

Typically, you'd replace service parts...

- After a set time has elapsed. Annually for example.
- After you've covered a set amount of distance. XYZ thousand miles for a car or truck for example.
- After the machine has used a set volume. XYZ thousand litres of fuel through a fuel filter for example.

- After a set amount of running time. XYZ thousand hours for a boat engine for example.

All the above intervals need adjusting if there are external mitigating influences; for example, unusually heavy use, or operating in extreme cold, heat, or in a dusty environment. All the above would mean shorter intervals in between replacement of service items. Air filters clog quickly in dusty desert environments for example.

All manufacturers publish instructions regarding maintenance and service intervals for consumable parts. Check your manuals or search online for specific service details for your stuff. Be aware also that not keeping to a manufacturer's maintenance schedule can invalidate any guarantee you might have in the first few years.

Of course, manufacturers will disagree, but you can extend the life of *some* service parts by dismantling and cleaning them. Especially on older, less valuable machines. For example, remove and blow air filters through with an airline to clean out dust and debris at least once on some machines (note I said 'some' here, please don't try this on your classic Ferrari!).

In general though, neglecting the replacement of service parts will have an adverse effect on the efficiency and performance of a machine. For example, the aforementioned clogged up air filter, will have been causing excessive fuel consumption as the engine would struggle to maintain the correct air to fuel ratio needed for maximum efficiency and performance. Similarly, a clogged dust filter on your vacuum cleaner makes the motor work harder and run hot, shortening its life.

TYPICAL SERVICE ITEMS

- **Oil filters**: Replaceable paper or cartridge types or cleanable metal screen types.
- **Air filters**: Replaceable paper types or foam types where you wash out the old oil and add new oil (squeezing out the excess).
- **Fuel filters**: Usually paper types replaceable at specific timed intervals.

- **Lubricants**: Remove old lube and replace (oil, grease, gearbox oil, transmission fluid, differential gear oil, etc).

- **Fluids**: Drain and replace old fluid (brake fluid, coolants, hydraulic fluid, etc.). Air conditioning fluid/ gas needs specialist equipment to replenish as it's dangerous stuff, for you and the environment.

- **Brake systems**: brake pads, brake disks, cylinder seals, brake fluid etc.; remove and replace when worn out or tired (brake fluid absorbs water and degrades over time).

- **Belts**: (and other drive mechanisms such as chains); usually replaced at specific intervals or when broken on non-critical stuff.

- **Seals**: O rings, gaskets etc. replace at specific intervals to prevent failures or leaks in use.

- **Drive**: Clutches and other drive plates. Replace when friction material wears away and drive starts to slip and or motion is lost.

- **Bushes**: Rubber or plastic isolation parts which cushion parts from one another under load. Replace when movement is excessive.

- **Electrical**: High voltage items need replacement at set intervals due to electrode wear. Includes brushes in motors, spark plugs in engines. Low voltage items such as batteries, replace when ineffective.

- **Tyres**: The tread or surface material wears away and once the built-in wear bars (solid bands or rubber which cross the tread) become visible, the tyre needs replacing (don't wait until you can see cloth...)

- **Bearings**: Hmm, are these service items or repairs? Either way, bearings are there to allow things to move without damaging expensive components. Some minimally worn bearings might last a little longer if cleaned out and repacked with grease. Once noisy or slack though, it's best to replace them to prevent seizure and damage to other components.

MAINTAINING DIFFERENT MATERIALS

Let's look at some basic maintenance you can do on just a few of the materials you'll find around your home. Some (but not all) materials have a surface finish or coating to prevent deeper damage from the elements or to protect it from contaminants.

Other materials, like masonry for example, don't have a coating as such, but still need protecting by taking some simple preventative measures, mostly related to keeping them as dry as possible... Remember, water is a pain in the derriere, and not just to tennis and cricket players...

The surface of any material is under attack all the time from a wide variety of factors... here are some of the 'enemies'...

- **Water**: A key ingredient to cause rust on ferrous metals. Even the moisture present in air causes problems, (×2 for water because it's that bad).

- **Air**: Contains the oxygen needed to create rust on ferrous metals in the presence of water. It also carries particles, chemical and physical which can damage surface finishes.

- **Sun**: Ultraviolet radiation causes UV degradation. Also causes thermal instability by expanding coatings and base materials at different rates which can cause cracking or separation (oh, and sunburn; ouch).

- **Heat**: Accelerates many chemical reactions between elements.
- **Cold**: Especially below freezing temperatures. Causes thickening of any lubrication, stiffness and thermal instability by shrinking coatings and base materials at different rates which can cause cracking or separation.
- **Chemicals**: Salts, acid rain, smoke, smog, oils and even sweat from your skin and the funk from grandad's pipe...
- **Friction**: Physical friction or movement can accelerate wear and tear on surface finishes.
- **Careless use**: Causes damage such as scratches, chips & dents.

Once unprotected, (even if only by a tiny bit) most things outside eventually rot, corrode, erode, degrade, or discolour, even so called 'no maintenance' plastic. To guard against this damage, always keep any finishes and coatings 100% intact to protect the underlying material. Plus, it's important to re-apply finishes before the original finish fails completely and starts flaking away or you'll have much more work to do.

All materials react differently to exposure to the elements...

- Timber will rot or attract bacteria or bugs which feed on it. Damp wood is a bug magnet (just ask any bug)! Dry wood lasts centuries.
- Masonry goes soft and crumbly or spalls.
- Ferrous metal containing iron rusts or oxidises extensively because iron oxide is not protective.
- Non-ferrous metal such as aluminium, copper, brass, lead, tin, zinc etc. don't rust, but can corrode, discolour, oxidise, or react to other metals. Some oxides are protective, e.g. the green coating on copper.

- Metal alloys such as brass, bronze, pewter or stainless steel also don't rust, but can corrode, discolour, oxidise, or react to other metals. Most oxides are protective though.
- Plastic discolours, degrades, or goes brittle, sometimes this only affects the surface.
- Rubber goes hard, perishes and splits.
- Fabrics rot, disintegrate, go stiff or tear easily. Think tents, covers, coats, etc.

Most of the above materials have some kind of protective finish that needs maintenance or topping up periodically. Let's take a look at the specific things you can do to a few different materials...

PROPER PREPARATION BEFORE REPLACING FINISHES

I'll put this here, before we look at specific materials as the principles are similar whether you're maintaining a wall, woodwork, or a metal gutter. Preparation is critical, just slapping on new stuff simply won't protect the material, even if it looks good initially. Generally...

- Scrape away any old flaky layers of the old finish.
- Clean down with a 'house cleaner' detergent, with a mould killer element if there are green or black spores on the surface.

  A bucket of cleaner and another of clean water and a couple of sponges work well indoors. Wipe over with one sponge and detergent and 'rinse' with the other sponge and clean water. Outdoors, careful use of a pressure washer to pump cleaner onto the surface works well (don't go too close). Scrub with a small brush on a long handle and afterwards rinse everything away being careful with the angle you use (avoid getting water behind anything), mimic how the rain would hit the surface to be safe. Allow plenty of time for everything to dry.

- Sand down the surface, removing any 'shine' to provide a rock-solid base (called 'key') for new coatings.

- Use a suitable primer on any bare areas, maybe even two coats (if applicable). Lightly sand with a fine sandpaper to flatten again.
- The final sanding grade should be 120/180 grit (or finer) otherwise the scratch marks may show through the final finish.
- Apply the finish coats following the manufacturer's instructions (usually two for best durability).
- Lightly sand in between coats with fine sandpaper and work in a super clean environment for time consuming, but glass smooth results.

Cleaning, scraping and sanding before painting prevents your hard work looking like this after a relatively short time.

If you can't identify the existing finish, you should ask your local supplier for advice because some finishes are not compatible with each other. Try to take in a sample if possible, remove a small opening window frame or a small drawer front for example.

The world of paint is getting complicated. Gone are the old days of water-based paint for the wall and oil for woodwork. There is a water-based paint for all situations nowadays. Oil is still the most durable in my opinion, but the long drying times and high odour is a problem many folks won't tolerate any more. I haven't used oil-based paints in a client's house for years. Oil is still popular for external works though.

It used to be common to 'thin' or add a little extra to paint, (water to water-based paint, white spirit to oil paint etc.), to make them flow better and go a little further. But these days you need to be careful to follow the manufacturers recommendations, especially regarding thinning, as many don't allow it, chemically.

Be aware that there are a few timber species that are naturally rot resistant like cedar, chestnut, white oak, douglas fir, larch, redwood, or cypress and you'll see these used without further protection.

A note about any sealants you find between differing neighbouring materials. Flexible sealants are critical to stop water penetrating gaps because the material behind any sealant you find is often poorly protected against damp. Door and window frames for example may only have a coat of primer on the parts of the frame you can't see. Water that gets past these sealants and into the nooks & crannies around the frame/timber can hang around, eventually causing decay. Check each year to make sure your sealant hasn't dried out leaving gaps. Silicone sealant is a popular (but poor) choice here, but paintable 'mastic,' or other non-setting type is preferable. You *cannot* paint silicone, which makes future decorating difficult.

TIMBER MAINTENANCE

Internal conditions are usually too dry for timber used internally on door, skirting boards, architraves, and trims etc. to decay. Maintenance is limited to re-decorating when the originals become dirty or out of date.

However, it's worth checking regularly any timber or trims situated close to external doors, washbasins, showers, baths, washing machines and dishwashers etc. for early signs of damp because of a problem with the finish or indeed from leaks from any of the above appliances etc.

Some internal timber finishes require specific cleaning and polishing with dedicated chemicals, French polishing on fine furniture for example.

Most other timber is bare and unprotected, with the exception of timber designed to live outside permanently like fencing or decking products (which are pressure impregnated with a green or brown preservative). Most of the timber inside your house stays in this bare state and needs no further protection (unless you suspect a pest problem like woodworm). Examples would be; floor joists, stud walls, roof timbers and floorboards.

When you see bare timber in your home (in the attic for example), it's worth looking out for signs of new insect activity, especially in the spring and summer. Look out for small holes and 'frass' (bug poo basically, which looks a bit like fine sawdust).

Also, look for any white stains, which could indicate a water leak, especially around any valley (sloping upwards between two different parts of the roof), gully (flat junctions between two roof sections), chimneys or other abutments. Be especially vigilant looking for evidence of insects if you find any damp timber in your home. Most wood boring insects don't like dry conditions, but they go absolutely gaga for slightly damp timber... it's heaven to them (it's easier to chew you see).

Protect all exposed and untreated timber outside, such as window frames, door frames and timber trims with several coats of paint or other timber preservative such as varnish, timber stain, wax, oil, or other chemical preservative. You should expect to re-apply most types of finishes at set intervals to maintain protection against decay. Re-application intervals range from a few years in locations exposed to wind and rain or near the coast, to a decade or more in sheltered locations and elevations (not facing prevailing weather).

Also, whilst treated or impregnated timber doesn't technically need any extra protection, giving it some is not going to hurt. I'm old enough now that I'm seeing treated timber I installed more than 25 years ago showing definite signs of decay. Ensure you use a treatment suitable for impregnated timber.

Check your timber in the springtime once the weather warms up, look for...

- **Flaking, lifting, or peeling**: Caused by several things, poor preparation prior to applying the finish, or just weather and time.

- **Crazing and cracking**: Surface looks like alligator or crocodile skin. Could be because of poor preparation prior to applying the finish, mismatched product types, or an adverse reaction to older product (i.e. a hard oil paint over a softer water-based paint), or just too many layers because of extreme old age.

- **Blistering or bubbles**: Could be poor preparation again (are you starting to see a pattern with this? Hint, the majority of problems are caused by poor preparation... just sayin'), but also trapped moisture or solvent in between coats or even because the paint was applied in the sunshine and the outer layer dried too quick.

- **Chalking**: Where aging finishes, usually in exposed areas dries to a dusty surface over time.

- **Mildew or mould**: Usually in damp areas that don't get a lot of sunshine. Needs cleaning with a cleaner formulated to combat the spores. Spray on with a pump-up garden sprayer and leave to soak and usually rinse off with water. But read the instructions first!

- **Dried out**: Look out for timber which has a really dry surface. Some timber preservatives really soak into the surface and over time leaves them looking washed or dried out.

MASONRY MAINTENANCE

Masonry is durable stuff... if it's able to dry out easily after getting wet or frozen. Long periods spent wet and/or frozen will quickly cause damage. The absolute best way to protect all types of masonry is to keep it as dry as possible; it's as simple as that. Sounds unlikely I know, it's a wall; *but*, preventing *any* wall getting excessively wet will prolong its life considerably.

Minimise unnecessary water from soaking into your masonry by making sure everything is doing its job and there is only one way to do this, yup, you've got to watch it, live, in action... when it's pouring down with rain, the harder the better. No good waiting until it stops, all the interesting stuff is over by then. Next time it pours down with rain, 'suit up', don your sou'wester or grab an umbrella and go and take a slow walk around your property (ignore the strange looks from the neighbours!) and watch to see where all that water is going, you'll learn lots, or nothing. Both is good; well, one isn't really, as it does mean you have a problem, but look at it on the bright side, at least you now know what the problem is...

Start at the top and ensure the roof is doing its job and *all* the water is running off the roof and into the guttering properly and that the gutter isn't overflowing. Check it doesn't dribble back from the roof edge, missing the gutter completely and run down the wall.

Check the amount of 'splash back' (water that bounces up onto the wall from hard paved surfaces). Ideally the ground level is (at least) 150mm (6") down from your Damp Proof Course (DPC). Make sure any paving at the base of walls drains away from the wall too and doesn't puddle next to the wall. It's a great idea to have a 300mm (12") loose gravel 'buffer' between any hard paving and the wall (or a small soil border with ground cover type plants) as this also stops rainwater bouncing up the wall. It still needs to be at least 150mm (6") down from your DPC though.

You'll find the DPC around the base of your house, usually underneath the bottom of the door frames. On older homes this may consist of (one to three) courses of especially hard bricks like blue bricks or red engineering bricks, with or without a thin layer of lead sheet on top. On more modern homes, it's an impermeable layer of bituminous felt or plastic etc. You might be able to see the plastic or felt damp proof course as a thin black line in the horizontal mortar joint at the same level as the bottom of the doorframes. If not, it's probably just behind the surface of the mortar joint.

Any freestanding garden walls need effective cappings (on top) incorporating a means of stopping the water from running down onto the face of the wall. This is usually a groove cut or cast into the underside of concrete copings (called a drip) or nibs on projecting tiles bedded underneath hard bricks etc. The drip allows water to fall away from the face of the wall. Try watching the water running off the capping of the wall when it's raining hard. Ideally, the top part of a wall should have a damp-proof course underneath the capping material as well, but many tradesmen fear that vandals will easily disturb the capping, so it's unusual to find one.

A word about sealing your masonry to keep water out. Hmm, some folks love it and others will tell you it'll sound the death knell for your poor wall. Personally, I think it will end badly if the wall has underlying damp issues. If water is getting into the wall, it must find a way out and if you seal the surface.... yup, it's going to cause damage somewhere as the moisture fights to find a way out.

However, if you've a wall that's rained on whatever you do, or a chimney getting a beating every time it rains, then by all means go for a breathable silicone treatment, with one caveat. Do it at the end of the summer after a long, long period of dry weather to ensure the brickwork is bone dry to start with. To stop water getting into the wall, consider covering it up for a while (with an air gap to allow evaporation) before treating it. Always follow the instructions as products vary and find one that's breathable for best results.

In addition to protecting your masonry from water, you'll need to check it annually for movement damage. Large cracks can be serious if caused by *subsidence* which is movement associated with damage from nearby large trees or leaking drains. Minor *settlement* cracking is less serious if caused by the 'normal' settling in of a house over time. There are several situations which can lead to movement and subsequent cracking. Look out for...

- **Zig zag cracks**: These follow the joints, running across your walls, usually low down. Either 'live' or active and moving; or old and stable. Monitor to determine by using 'tell tales' fixed across the cracks (google it!). Log your readings over time.

- **Shear cracks**: Straight cracks running up through the bricks and joints; they are always serious. Might indicate a design fault or movement needing attention. Imagine the stress it takes to break fully bedded bricks in mortar. Not good... Monitor as with the zig-zag cracks above.

- **Large trees**: (esp. close to walls). These suck up lots of water drying out the ground, shrinking it. The amount of water varies with the seasons causing the soil to shrink and swell, pushing against the masonry. Roots also eventually grow big enough to push against walls and into gaps or cracks where they act like a jack, forcing things apart.

- **Tree stumps**: (esp. close to walls). Large trees take up a lot of water, if removed, the water that once went into the tree causes the soil to swell and 'heave' up, pushing against the masonry.

- *NOTE*: I know, the two scenarios, above right? Catch 22 huh! Deciding whether to leave a tree or take it out depends on any evident damage caused, go with the lesser evil.

- **Leaking drains**: Could be leaking for years before anyone notices. A leak saturates surrounding soil and washes it into the drain and away, undermining the pipe itself and any nearby hardstanding or walls. Look for sunken areas of garden or paving or leaning or sagging walls.

- **Rainwater systems**: Leaking rainwater systems saturate and destabilise the soil around the base of walls. Make sure your rainwater is going where it's supposed to.

- **Distortion**: Watch out for difficulties when opening windows or doors. This might indicate wall movement (or just old/ poor joinery).

- **Efflorescence**: Look for white, salty deposits on the wall, often just above ground level and up to about 1m (3') high. These are soluble salts left behind when water evaporates from a damp wall. Brush them off and carry out further investigation to rectify the cause of the damp.

Some masonry outdoors ends up covered in render (sometimes called stucco). Render is plastering outside basically. This maybe by design from the outset or applied as an attempt to tidy up (read cover-up) a wall in poor condition (with spalled bricks etc.). Covering poor walls with render rarely works because the source of damp damaging the bricks in the first place, if not rectified, will carry on, eventually blowing the render off the wall as well.

Check render annually...

- As with bare masonry, look for wavy lines of white salty marks or deposits on the first metre (3') from the ground. Often means water is in the wall and evaporating out through the render, leaving the soluble salts behind.

- Gently tap with a short stick or piece of wood and listen for hollow areas where the render has separated slightly from the wall. Hollow sounding areas are a sign water is behind the render and freezing/ expanding.

- Look for actual bulges and bumps which are another sign water is behind the render and freezing (thus swelling and causing the bumps).

- Look at the edges, corners, bottom etc. where there might be metal trims going rusty and blowing off the render.

- Look at the bottom edge if it's near the ground, does it cover the damp proof course? Render should NEVER cross the damp proof course as it would allow damp to run straight up the wall.

- Look for hairline cracks or spalled areas which will let water penetrate, wetting the wall inside. Fill any cracks with outdoor flexible filler and re-paint.

- Look for spalled, crumbly, or missing areas which will let water penetrate, wetting the wall inside. Chop away the damage and re-render.

- Check any paint coverings for integrity and durability.

- Check any texturing for integrity (Tyrolean, roughcast or pebble-dash etc.) Poor quality stuff literally falls off when lightly touched with a paint scraper etc. Replace coating as necessary.

One last comment regarding walls, as attractive as it can look on certain properties, it's probably best to avoid growing creeping plants up your walls. Although creepers are unlikely to damage the brickwork itself, they can certainly damage doors, windows, guttering and your roof. If you insist on creepers, make sure you cut them back annually at least 300mm (12") from all the above-mentioned areas, especially at the roofline. You could also consider growing them up a trellis instead of directly on the wall.

Oh, and p.s. *genuine* rising damp is less common than you think. Help old walls by restoring them to their original breathable condition (i.e. no cement!) and managing the water at the top and the bottom of the wall and you might just find you don't have a rising damp problem after all... (Woo hoo! Crack open that Champagne!).

PLASTER MAINTENANCE

Maintain internal plaster by wiping it free of marks as they happen and re-painting every few years after washing down and filling any dents or scrapes etc. with a decorator's filler and a quick sand flat. High traffic areas like hallways and entrances might need decorating every 3 years and low traffic areas like spare bedrooms every 10 or even 15 years.

ROOF MAINTENANCE

Roofs are generally maintenance free, anything you need to do to a roof is really a repair and that's a different book. That said, you should check the roof regularly and clear away anything you find growing on the roof such as moss, weeds, or even small trees (believe me, especially in valleys, chimney back gutters, central gutters etc.).

On a nice day, grab or borrow a pair of binoculars and head out to a spot where you can see most of the roof. If you have access to a ladder and understand you should have someone stood on the bottom of it and somewhere to tie off the top to, then by all means go up to gutter level and take a closer look. Either way, check for the following...

- Missing ridge tiles (the ones right on the top or apex).
- Missing, cracked, askew or loose roof tiles.
- Missing mortar or tiles at the edges of the roof.
- Missing or disturbed flashings around chimneys, windows, skylights, pipes, or anything else penetrating the roof.
- Missing or disturbed flashings at abutments, parapet walls or adjacent properties etc.
- Cracked or damaged valleys or central gutters or troughs.

Any damage you see or find needs immediate repair, even if you don't yet see any sign of water getting inside the house. Roofs are amazing in their capacity to soak up water in the timbers, insulation etc. before it leaks into the room below. The longer you leave it, the more repairs you'll have to do. It's much better to replace a slipped tile or two than to replace rotten roof members, I do both regularly and I know which is cheapest...

PIPE MAINTENANCE

Pipes coming into the house don't usually need any maintenance other than to isolate and/or insulate any exposed to the cold in the winter time (think, outside taps in the garden) but the pipes going out of the house are another matter. Predictably these pipes carry all sorts of horrible stuff. Sticky stuff, greasy stuff, and stuff they shouldn't be carrying at all, (think plastic, shaving gear, non-bio degradable stuff and even dead pets etc. Oh, and latex stuff, you know what I mean? Yup, don't put those in the toilet either).

Two golden rules. Only stuff you have eaten plus toilet paper in the toilet and never put oils or grease in the sink. *These rules are unbreakable* (just think of the folks at the end of the pipe...).

Toilets block easily when stuff snags up at joints, bends, or poorly constructed parts of the system etc. Even something small will attract other stuff like tissue paper building up and up until the pipe blocks completely and water backs up the pipe. In sinks, oil and grease solidify when they hit the cold pipe further down and will build up over time. Wipe greasy pans with kitchen paper and store used cooking oils responsibly, i.e. in an old 5L plastic container and periodically recycle it (google 'fatbergs' to really freak yourself out).

The blocking process can happen over several days as pipes in the ground have a considerable capacity. Once a toilet starts to fill up, it's time to grab a special toilet plunger. Place the plunger in the bowl and pump up and down, this pushes the water and air in the trap back and forth and may dislodge a small obstruction... maybe, but probably not.

More likely you'll need to head out into the yard and check your access points (inspection chambers or IC in the UK, formerly manholes). If the first one is full of, erm, water (hint, it won't just be water...) head down to the next access point and so on. Repeat until you are at an access point which is empty. If they are all full between you and the main sewer in the street, then the blockage is in the last section of pipe between your last access point and the main sewer (or in the main sewer itself, canvas neighbours to see if they have a problem. Blocked main sewers are the local authority's responsibility).

To clear a blocked drain, scrape around the edges of the covers over the access points with an old knife or trowel. Remove any screws (if any). If there are 'key' holes, go and buy a cheap set of drain keys, insert, turn 90º and heave. Otherwise, using a couple of prying implements (small pry bars, old flat screwdrivers, thick scrapers etc), gently work around the edge and lever the cover up. If really stuck, try tapping with a rubber mallet as well as getting progressively more aggressive with your levering. Never use a metal hammer, because cast iron covers are brittle and easily broken and steel ones dent. Scrape out and wire brush any rusty frame grooves and the edges of the cover. Put grease in the frame groove to make this easy next time.

Right, now you're ready to go 'drain diving'. Put old waterproofs on and duct tape the tops of some rubber gloves to the jacket and grab a set of drain rods (cheap, especially when compared to calling out a plumber). Pop the screw attachment on and place the rod in the pipe 'upstream' towards the full IC. Keep screwing rods on until you hit the blockage. Twist the screw into the blockage and push/pull. You'll feel the blockage clear and hear the rumble of water coming from 'upstream', (hint: time to bug out!). Let the build-up of sewage flow away and clear.

Always use drain rods carefully and *always be slowly turning the rods clockwise* as you push them in and draw them out. NEVER go anticlockwise *ever*, or you'll 'unscrew' a section and lose rods in the drain (then you're in even more trouble).

Once you've cleared the main blockage run a hose pipe down the drain (from the first access point) or flush the loo several times to help clear any remaining debris and to keep the debris moving until it's in the main sewer. A bucket or three of screaming hot, soapy water down the toilet won't do any harm either... Oh, you might need a hot shower too, at this point...

You'll only need to do the above once, before you learn your lesson to never put stuff into drains that have no business being there...

Lastly the guttering needs checking (and yes, I know a gutter is only a 'half' pipe!). Empty it of leaves and other debris which builds up over the year. After the autumn, once all the leaves have dropped is as good a time as any to do this, even if it is a little cold by then. Working safely from a ladder, scrape and brush the debris into a bucket. It is usually difficult (in the UK at least) as the roof tiles get in the way.

During your annual 'pouring with rain' inspection, check along the length of the gutter run and especially the end opposite the downpipe to ensure it's not spilling over the top of the gutter (especially at the back where it's difficult to spot) during heavy rain.

Check the downpipes for blockages (check especially any bends, top or bottom) which cause the pipe to fill up and leak from joints above the blockage. If there are no blockages but the down pipe still leaks, check the pipe for splits and that the joints are the right way around; i.e. male part into female part etc. I know, I know I dislike the crude terms too, but it's accurate. Oh, and don't google it either, (shudders), if you want to learn more, check out this page... en.wikipedia.org/wiki/Gender_of_connectors_and_fasteners.

METAL MAINTENANCE

All bare metals react when exposed to the environment. Metals such as aluminium and stainless steel create a microscopic protective oxide layer which effectively stops further corrosion (lucky them) making it not strictly necessary to paint them. Other metals such as steel and iron are not so lucky and corrode extensively in the right conditions, namely in the presence of water and air. Areas of bare steel or iron will start to rust in a few hours or even quicker in ideal conditions.

Other factors such as salt (from the road or in the sea air) or acid rain, act as accelerators, worsening corrosion. One last factor to be aware of in the presence of salty air/water, is adverse reactions between different metals (such as stainless steel and aluminium) called *galvanic reaction or corrosion.* In plain language, this is an electrical reaction (not dissimilar to what goes on inside a battery) and causes severe corrosion; as anyone who owns an old Land Rover knows (they have aluminium bodies and steel chassis). Check any paint, coatings, sealants, or tapes keeping apart different metals and replace them if showing signs of failing.

Maintaining metal finishes falls into two parts; preventing contaminants damaging the coating and repairing any physical damage that occurs.

First then, finishes and coatings on most ferrous metal, (iron and steel stuff that rusts) living outside are under constant attack from potentially harmful contaminants, which damage the surface over time. In broadly alphabetical order, contaminants range from acid rain, ash and soot, bird droppings, building dust like cement or plaster, fingerprints, grit, rail dust (microscopic metal particles created by decay, vehicles, industry, oh and trains, hence the term), spilled fuel, splattered bugs, tar, tree sap, all the way to water, which leaves behind 'hard to shift' deposits when it dries out. Even the ultra violet rays found in lovely sunshine will damage some coatings believe it or not. The paint on older, red, and yellow cars is particularly vulnerable to serious fading caused by ultra violet rays if not regularly protected by polish. Even silly things, like writing "clean me" in gritty road dust on a friend's car will introduce microscopic scratches and mark the finish.

Fortunately, as mentioned earlier in this chapter, the answer is tediously simple. You must clean contaminants off your metal finishes more-or-less as they happen. Bird droppings for example are chemically nasty, but the real problem (found by vehicle cleaning experts Autoglym) is the way paint expands and contracts in the sunshine. Anything sitting on the paint as the sun warms and softens the layers, risks becoming microscopically embedded into the coating as it cools. You can imagine, paint has a pretty tough job as it is, trying to stay attached to a piece of thermally dynamic metal. Here in Norway for example, the temperature ranges from minus 30°C to plus 30°C, that's a whopping 60°C of expansion and contraction the paint must cope with, without coming unstuck, (which I think is amazing).

Fortunately, there is a silver lining to cleaning your metalwork finishes... it is an ideal time to spot the second problem; *damage* to coatings.

Keep a constant eye open for physical damage when cleaning. Don't ignore any small damage to finishes because the corrosion process on steel for example is so very fast. Look out for...

- Small chips; often small but deep 'holes' caused by flying debris like stones. Repair with a tiny drop of matching paint on the very tip of a cocktail stick or toothpick. The paint flows into the chip and flattens out almost perfectly; brushes, even tiny ones tend to just smear the paint all over the place. Use nail polish in a pinch.

- Scratches; repair with a like-for-like propriety product or cover with something that repels water to keep out the elements. On less visually important stuff, silicone or bitumen products are common or wax polish in a pinch.

- Dents on their own are not too troublesome if they are shallow, but often dents crease the metal and creases are likely to 'crack' finishes, lifting the coating from the metal, letting in the elements with predicable results. Scrape away loose stuff and refinish with your chosen paint.

- Flaking, lifting, or peeling finishes; caused by several things, poor preparation prior to painting, stressed or excess movement of the metal or a result of weather and time. Scrape, sand and refinish.

- Crazing and cracking, (paint surface looks like alligator or crocodile skin). Could be because of poor preparation prior to painting, mismatched paint types, or an adverse reaction to older paint (i.e. hard paint over softer paint), the metal could be too thermally active hot/cold, or too many layers of paint and/or extreme old age. Scrape, sand and refinish.

- Blistering or bubbles; could be poor preparation again (are you starting to see a pattern with this? Hint, 65% of paint problems are down to poor preparation… just sayin'), but it could also be moisture or solvent trapped in between coats or even because the paint was applied in the sunshine and the outer layer dried too quick. Scrape, sand down and refinish.

- Chalking; where aging paint, usually in exposed spots dries to a dusty surface over time. Sand and refinish.

- Mould; usually in damp areas that don't get a lot of sunshine. Needs thorough cleaning with a cleaner formulated to combat the spores. Spray on with a pump-up garden sprayer and leave to

maintaining different materials

soak and usually rinsing off with water. Read the instructions first! Then sand down and refinish.

- Faded coatings; can become micro porous and lose its ability to protect letting in contaminants like water etc. Protect faded paint temporarily with a lot of polish. Otherwise, sand down and refinish with your chosen paint.

- Rough paint; paint on vehicles will 'collect' lots of tiny metal particles called rail dust (all vehicles produce tiny metal dust particles in use, originally from train wheels/tracks etc., hence the term). Thrown up off the road they embed themselves into the paints surface. Rub your hand over the paint surface to feel them. Wash, and gently rub a well lubricated 'clay bar' over the paint to remove them. Re-apply waxes and polish as the surface will be totally clean/bare. (p.s. clay bars will blow you away...).

Repair any small damage with a suitable matching product straight away. Aim to prevent minor damage like scratches or chips in paint or other coatings from getting any worse. Because get worse they definitely will, 100% guaranteed. Water will creep into every little crevice and start its deadly work.

Re-coat any areas showing signs of weather or wear. You can buy all kinds of paint for metal; from small touch-up bottles incorporating a tiny brush up to paint suitable for spraying. Head for your local car parts supplier and DIY paint stores for more info.

It's essential you maintain any finish before the existing protection degrades or starts to fail. Once the paint starts to show the metal beneath, its game over and the only answer is to get right back to a sound surface and re-apply the coating. Arguably then, this is not maintenance but a repair.

It's possible to stabilise neglected and rusty metal with special rust stabilising chemicals from your local motoring supplies store.

You can even paint straight onto rust (if it's clean, dry, scraped and properly wire brushed first) with special paints such as Hammerite, which is available in a smooth or dimpled (hammered) finish. Search online for 'hammered paint' to find this kind of paint near you.

Protect inaccessible areas using a wax-based compound via a spray or pump lance. Simply thread the lance into holes, gaps, behind panels etc and spray the wax liberally in all directions as you draw it out. The wax will creep into crevices and can 'self-repair' minor damage from stones and scratches etc. Waxoyle is a well-known brand in Europe, search for "corrosion protection products" to find something similar in your area or visit an auto supplies store. Cheap endoscopes are available to plug into your laptop, making it easy to check inside hidden areas (e.g. inside structural members under vehicles).

Arguably, you can use anything that repels water for rough protection on less critical things like lawn mowers and so on. Things like silicone sealant, waxes, polish, waterproof tapes, waterproof glues, or adhesives and even oil or grease. However, don't do this if you intend to paint the item in the future, as paint adhesion will be a problem; use a rust stabilising primer instead.

You can polish some metals with wax based or special polymers to provide extra protection, but in fact, you're protecting the life of the metals protective layer, i.e. the paint! However, this mostly applies to vehicles, for some reason, folks never want to polish their metal drainpipes, gates, lampposts etc. even though it would prolong the life of their coatings...

RUST AS A FINISH

Some heavy items of metal don't need additional protection and function quite happily with a layer of corrosion (rust or iron oxide). This doesn't cause a problem because the items are so very thick or solid that corrosion is too slow to cause loss of function during their expected lifespan (brake callipers and some suspension parts on vehicles for example.)

Rust is also becoming an acceptable 'finish', mostly on street furniture and art, where by design, the metal is thick enough to avoid structural weakening by corrosion over time.

Unprotected non-ferrous metals (stuff like gold, silver, copper, and aluminium) don't rust like steel, but can tarnish and discolour when exposed to the air. Use a special, mildly abrasive metal polish to clean and maintain a shiny finish. The abrasive action removes tarnish, sulphates, and oxides, at the same time protecting against further tarnishing by excluding air and moisture. You can restore brass, chrome, aluminium, gold, silver etc., from a very tarnished condition repeatedly. Be wary of plated items (microscopic layer of valuable metal over a cheap base metal) though as over polishing with abrasive polish can rub completely through the thin plating if you go bananas.

Sometimes though, the development of a patina is desirable. Copper used as a roofing material for example; often left to develop a characteristic blue-green tint. Note, it can take many years in some locations for the thin layer of copper sulphate to develop. There are chemicals to accelerate the process towards green, as well as waxes or oils to prevent it, keeping the shiny copper look, (you pays your money and you makes your choice...).

PLASTIC MAINTENANCE

Most everyday plastics only need an occasional wipe over with a damp cloth or mild detergent to remove potential contaminants. As with wood and metal, removing potentially corrosive things like bird faeces or potentially acidic chemicals in soot or carbon is a good idea. Plus, the surface of most types of plastic is relatively soft and easily scratched by abrasive dust and grit.

Some types of plastic discolour when exposed to the suns UV rays over time and may eventually become brittle or show signs of surface degradation. It's possible to slow down this damage by regularly using a proprietary plastic protector, which will clean, restore any faded colour, and protect against further discolouration. Most plastic living outside would need regular application to maintain protection and looks; although to be honest most people don't bother because they believe plastic to be maintenance free.

For example, some of the black plastics used on vehicle trims and bumpers etc eventually turn grey over time. Using a proprietary plastic restorer like 'Back to Black' (or similar) will restore the original colour fairly successfully and regular application will build up a protective layer.

RUBBER MAINTENANCE

Once considered an old-fashioned weak and friable material, with the addition of many different elements, rubber has morphed into a modern, high performing, hi-tech composite material. Adding synthetic compounds, fillers, reinforcing strands of metal, cloth, or fibre, has made it stronger, better at handling temperature extremes and much more durable. For example, drive-belts containing strong threads or fabrics to help limit stretch and resist breaking strains, now last for many thousands of hours with minimal wear. Tyres also contain miles of reinforcing fabric and steel wires or bands.

However, age comes to us all, and exposure to sunlight, extreme heat or cold, chemicals, friction and excessive stretching or compression eventually causes rubber stuff to perish or fail, either slowly or catastrophically. Perished rubber looks 'dried out' and shows crazing on the surface. Perished rubber can keep going for a while, but as you can't tell how deep the perishing goes, you should replace anything severely perished as soon as possible to prevent serious failures. This especially applies to tyres on vehicles, although arguably, you don't need to panic about your wheelbarrow!

Because rubber leads such a demanding life it's difficult to protect, but there is one thing we can do to help, we can try to shield it from the worst of the elements. For example, UV rays will damage tyres (especially those not regularly used), turning them grey as the 'carbon black' UV stabiliser gets older and less effective. Seriously consider covering up tyres on stuff you only use occasionally like trailers, motorhomes, RV's, boat trailers, classic cars, and the like, to keep sunshine off the rubber, they'll last longer if you do.

Using your tyres also helps protective waxes built into the tyre; migrate to the surface, protecting them from things like the naturally occurring Ozone in the air, (a great excuse to take out your toys, i.e. "I'm just maintaining the tyres dear, I'll be back in a couple of hours...").

There are various rubber conditioners you can use to top up this built-in protection and slow down deterioration. Spray or wipe the conditioner on tyres, window seals, door seals and weather seals etc. Rubber conditioners have been somewhat controversial of late, so look for brands that specifically state they include UV protection. These should be available from your local motor supplies store.

> Rubber seals called 'O' rings can fail and leak.
>
> They are called 'O' rings because when they leak you'll often hear "O shoot, that seals gone!"
>
> Just kidding, it's because they're round like an 'O'...

Rubber O rings are round seals (or square/ rectangular/ oval/ etc.!) to stop liquids (or air) from leaking, they either go inside a pipe in a groove (e.g. pipe joints) or outside a pipe in a groove (e.g. quick fit hosepipe connectors)

These rubber rings harden over time, cracking or even splitting into several pieces causing dripping or full-blown leaks. Checking and making sure they are properly lubricated helps maintain a good seal and protects the rubber O ring itself.

(assuming you don't live on the sofa!), you have ideal conditions for excess wear and tear.

Fabric worn next to the skin also of course soaks up sweat, which is mildly corrosive to many natural fibres, (yuck a doodle...).

Sweat is corrosive as this rather gross old work hat shows

Waterproof fabrics are a little more complicated as there are several different types. Maintenance varies from reapplying an oil or wax to spraying with a water repelling chemical and some you simply wash in a washing machine on a special setting. Read the manufacturers label to find out what type of fabric it is; always follow any aftercare instructions and contact them if you can't read the label anymore, as getting this wrong can remove the fabrics waterproofing properties completely.

MAINTENANCE SCHEDULES

Many people, especially when on a budget, adopt a 'don't fix what isn't broken' approach to things (and that's fine for your toaster). However, when it comes to vehicles or checking your gutters etc., there's sense in sticking to a proper maintenance schedule. Because if you do, you'll avoid breakdowns and failures. If that's not enough, remember this; when it comes to selling something on, well maintained stuff (with receipts or records to prove it) sells quicker and for a higher price. Plus, prospective future purchasers of your stuff might easily walk away if they suspect there has been any neglect, (there are plenty more out there after all).

Consider drawing up your own maintenance schedule to record what you've done and what needs doing next. It doesn't have to be anything fancy; start with a simple list of jobs and when you aim to carry them out; either weekly, monthly, or annually, whatever fits your lifestyle.

Something popular with my well-heeled clients is to have several maintenance 'wish' lists; one for stuff they want to do this year, then another two lists with stuff they want to do within say five years and lastly a list for things they might want to do, but without a particular time frame (time and money permitting). All three are 'live' lists which you can amend continually.

How much you do and how often, depends on your location and each particular task or job (oh, and availability of time and cash of course!). However, as a general minimum, check your stuff before winter and then again in the spring. That way you avoid working when it's really cold and miserable plus you'll repair any small damage before the harsh winter weather sets in. Checking and doing a few maintenance spruce ups again in the spring also makes your stuff look good ready for the summer season (and doesn't waste valuable sunshine!).

Also, don't be a 'slave' to a schedule if the conditions don't warrant it. Maintaining something just because it is X years since you last maintained it, doesn't consider the current condition or 'need'. Regular checks will help you decide if it needs maintenance as planned in year X, or whether the recent harsh conditions means it needs redoing sooner, or the opposite; if recent mild conditions mean it can wait a little longer. Just-in-time maintenance is cost effective because it prevents neglect and gets the most out of your stuff.

If you have an older home, you could start by looking online for a great document from the conservation folks in Dublin called 'Maintenance: A Guide to the Repair of Older Buildings' just search ISBN 0-7557-7537-6 and look for the www.dublincity.ie domain to grab your free PDF copy.

UNSCHEDULED MAINTENANCE

Some things don't need a schedule because you do them on-the-spot or as you notice them. Often called the two-minute-rule; (keep a few tools in a handy drawer for just that).

Some examples of unscheduled maintenance...

- Loose stuff; e.g. a screw in a hinge on a cabinet door.
- Damage to vulnerable coatings; e.g. a stone chip on paint.

- Dry or stiff stuff needing lubrication; e.g. door hinge etc.
- New and unusual sounds need investigating immediately.
- Leaks of any kind, of any liquid, need immediate attention.
- Unusual smells need investigating immediately.
- Unusual vibrations; if it feels different; yup, it needs investigating right away.

VEHICLE MAINTENANCE

I wasn't sure whether to include this in this 'home' maintenance guide but a vehicle is a part of most folks lives these days, so I'll introduce it to you, in case you always thought it was something you should get someone else to do for you.

I'll not go into too much detail as the topic can fill books on its own, but I'll just tell you that although machines and vehicles are complex, most regular maintenance tasks are usually quite easy. Sure, occasionally you might need a special tool, but most are not particularly expensive to purchase, and most are easy enough to learn how to use via the instructions or by finding the 'go-to' guy for your vehicle on YouTube. I'm lucky, my everyday runabout is a Honda right now, so I have 'Eric the Car Guy' who is aptly named and a veritable font of info about my car (thanks Eric!).

You'll also need some easily found, specific technical information related to your vehicle (intervals between services etc., specifications for different fluids, tightness, or torque settings for fasteners etc.). This you can often find in the owner's handbook which comes with all machines, or find an independent one from someone like Haynes*. Libraries often have manuals for the most popular vehicles and there are lots available second hand online if you don't mind the odd oily fingerprint. These types of manuals and handbooks offer easy to follow maintenance information specific for your vehicle (this is the one-time step-by-step info is a good idea, as each car is essentially identical).

*Haynes.co.uk in the UK or Haynes.com internationally.

In addition to the manuals, there is a lot of video content online related to servicing (and repairing) vehicles; maybe because vehicle mechanics are more technically minded than most and like making videos?

Incidentally, whilst you're in the motor store you might also be able to get advice from their usually enthusiast staff (don't try this when they're busy though). Asking them to recommend a good product for a particular task is an easy way to break the ice.

If you own a vehicle you plan to keep a while, it's a good idea to find and join the owners club or forum for your vehicle. This is simply the best way to find solid maintenance information given freely from fellow fans of the marque. Search online for the vehicles name +owners club or +forum to start with. These guys often put lots of effort into posting about their own experiences along with lots of solutions for common problems on the forum.

I know searching forums is time consuming due to their size, but if you get the keywords right, you'll find really specific information. Don't let the information flow one-way either, if you fix something, post a quick note on the forum to help others. You're more likely to receive help yourself if you help others and earn some kudos. And definitely don't be the guy who signs up today and immediately begs for help, this makes you appear a more than a little rude. Don't be a 'taker', sign up and join in before you need to ask for help yourself. Even if it's just to say 'Hi, looking forward to joining in.' or to leave appreciative comments on other threads etc.

As always, the trick with vehicle maintenance is to study the parts in conjunction with reading through the steps FIRST. Repeatedly if necessary, until you're confident you understand at least how to begin the procedure. Also, make sure you have everything you need before you start (unless you have access to another car). There is nothing more annoying than partially dismantling something and then having to put them all back again to drive to the local motor store to pick up something you forgot...

And be prepared to get frustrated from time to time working on vehicles. Out of all the stuff I work on, fixing vehicles is the most likely one to annoy me. Either a component is very difficult to access, leading to skinned knuckles or worse; or something has corroded beyond reason and is proving very difficult to work on because it's seized solid. Imagine the two together, yup, it happens. All the time.

Sometimes you need to remove a lot of other things which are in the way to just see the darn thing which has broken; time consuming, tedious and there is always the risk of damaging something that was perfectly fine before you had to go in with the big hammers.

All I can say is, allow plenty of time, and make yourself as comfortable as possible. Use an old thin mattress to lay on and even something to support your head if you're underneath. Get the vehicle as high off the ground as you safely can, and I really do mean safely, people die underneath falling cars all the time... Invest in a good, high lift jack and strong axle stands to support the weight after you've jacked it up. Never work under a vehicle on a jack alone, death or serious injury beckons if you do.

Learn about rust and understand what causes it, it's the main Achilles heel on vehicles, it affects nearly everything. Buy a good anti-rust product by the gallon and don't be mean with it, spray it everywhere you can underneath, as we looked at before, rust often starts from the inside out, so get the stuff inside all those awkward to reach places. Oh and wear goggles underneath the car, or you'll get some of that rust in your eye, guaranteed!

Most folks running older vehicles adopt a 'if it's not broke, don't fix it' mentality and to be honest that's fine. Except when it comes to fluids. Even on the rattiest runabout, change the oil often, and check all the other liquids too; gearbox oils, steering fluid, coolant, brake fluid, and AC refrigerant to name a few. Keep moving parts greased and stop stone-chips from spreading with any water repelling stuff you have to hand (wax, Vaseline, clear nail polish etc).

HOME MAINTENANCE CHECKLIST 101

☑ **GOOD CONDITION**

☐ **SHOWING WEAR**

☐ **NEEDS ATTENTION**

I know right, finally we get to the 101 things on the darn checklist I promised on the cover of this book. My apologies, I just wanted to lay some foundations for you, to go over some of the things in this checklist and give you a little background knowledge to make sure you don't go off half cocked...

DON'T PUT OFF THE INEVITABLE

One last time, I promise. The earlier you spot potential home maintenance problems the quicker, easier, and cheaper it will be to fix them, thus protecting your most valuable asset. Read through the 101 things on this checklist and set aside some time to explore your home looking for potential maintenance problems, (you'll save time and money if you do...).

Draw up your own list of tasks to do and get to it! (there is a little space at the back of this book to get you started...).

And remember what we looked at a few minutes ago; it's a good idea to check your stuff before winter and then again in the spring. Coupled with the two-minute-rule for any tiny jobs, you're set to go.

I've labelled each item with one of the following four icons...

CHECK — This icon identifies something you need to check regularly to determine its condition or to identify a problem, failure, or weakness. Intervals depend on location.

TO DO — This icon outlines a brief plan or outline of work you can do to stop a problem in its tracks and also what to do to fix the problem if damage is already present.

TOP TIP — This icon gives you some extra information in the form of useful tips or tricks that I have learned or seen used to good effect on real building sites or during maintenance jobs.

CHOOSE LIFE — This icon gives you information highlighting something potentially dangerous. The skull is there for a reason! So many people are hurt each year carrying out DIY jobs at home. Some even die. Remember that no one ever intends to have an accident... so pay attention to these notes... your life may depend on it!

THE BIG OUTDOORS

HARD STANDING AREAS

[CHECK] Check that all the rainwater runs away and doesn't soak in or form puddles close to buildings or walls. Water that runs towards a wall or sits for long periods could easily find its way into the walls and eventually into the house.

[TO DO] Consider reconfiguring any hard-standing areas ensuring they slope away from your walls (called *fall*) towards drains or garden areas.

[CHECK] Check for any sunken paved or other areas where water pools after rain as these might indicate an erosion problem underneath the surface. look for possible causes of erosion, such as natural settlement of low weight bearing soils, insects such as ants, (or other digging critters!) settlement can also be a result of poor compaction of the sub-base under the hard-standing areas when it was built/laid.

Wheel ruts may also hold water after rain, as they are often very compact, but this does not necessarily mean there is a problem deeper in the ground. Leaking drains also cause soil erosion (see next section).

TO DO — You must repair or rectify the cause of any erosion before fixing damage to the hard-standing surface, otherwise the problem will re-occur in time. Typically, you'd lift or cut out the sunken areas. Add more substrate (sand/mortar/stone/soil/etc) and carefully level out. Replace surface material, tamping down and levelling up with the surrounding area using a timber straight edge or spirit level. Finish off joints with mortar or sand if applicable.

Check that rainwater isn't washing away any jointing material or surrounding soils, allowing water to easily get below the hard-standing rather than running off to the lawn or a drain etc

TOP TIP — Go and check your hard-standing areas during heavy rain or immediately after it stops, before water has a chance to soak in, or away.

DRAINS

CHECK — Check grills or grates for obvious blockages such as leaves and other debris which has washed down off the roof. Look underneath any grates as well because some always goes through, plus debris accumulates from stuff washed into sinks etc.

TO DO — Put your rubber gloves on and clear away anything sitting on top of grills/grates. Then lift out the grill/grate and scoop out anything sitting in the water trap, especially the one that takes water from the kitchen sink, and yes it will be very, very yucky...

TOP TIP — Put an old waterproof jacket on and get someone to duct tape the tops of rubber gloves to the jacket. This is a must if you're going proper 'drain diving' and especially if going into what's called 'foul' water pipes/drains (it's called foul for a reason...).

CHECK — Check that covers on any 'manholes', now called inspection chambers (IC) you have are free by removing them (in case of a blockage).

TO DO — Scrape around the edges of the IC cover with an old knife or trowel. Carefully remove any screws (if present). If there are 'key' holes, go and buy a cheap set of *drain keys*, insert them into the cleared-out holes, turn them 90º degrees and heave. If stuck (very, very likely) use a couple of prying implements (small pry bars, old flat screwdrivers etc), gently work around the edge and gradually lever the cover up. If it's really stuck, try tapping with a rubber mallet (or a short length of stout timber) as well as getting progressively more aggressive with your levering.

TOP TIP — Never, ever use a metal hammer to try and loosen a cast iron or plastic cover/frame, because they are quite brittle and easily broken. Galvanised steel ones (usually bright silver/grey in colour) are more forgiving, but will still dent if you go crazy.

CHECK — Check the chambers underneath the covers are clean (well, clean ish!) and free from detritus. If there is tissue paper etc. sitting on the concrete or plastic 'drain benching' higher up, this might mean the chamber is filling up occasionally and draining away slowly (one to keep an eye on...).

TO DO — If there is any mess or any build-up of crud inside the IC in the chamber, brush, hosepipe or gently pressure wash it away (don't go too close with a pressure washer, it'll damage the mortar). Soaking dried on crud, waiting a while and then rinsing works well.

TOP TIP — Believe it or not, drains shouldn't smell too bad if they are working properly. Seriously. Don't forget you could always consider hiring a drain camera to inspect the internal condition of your drains properly if you suspect there's a problem somewhere.

CHECK — Check each IC to see if there is water/nasty stuff sitting in the half pipe in the bottom. If present, you might have a blockage somewhere, (or the pipe has a very shallow fall or there might be a dip in the drain system, if it was poorly installed or has settled for example).

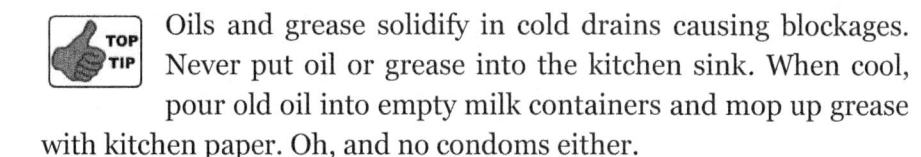

TOP TIP Oils and grease solidify in cold drains causing blockages. Never put oil or grease into the kitchen sink. When cool, pour old oil into empty milk containers and mop up grease with kitchen paper. Oh, and no condoms either.

TO DO If the IC is full of water however, then a pipe is definitely blocked 'downstream'. You can clear pipe blockages using a cheap set of 'drain rods'. Be warned, it's not the nicest job in the world...

When using drain rods to clear blockages, go gently and always be turning the rods clockwise as you push them in and draw them out. Then you won't 'lose' any because they came 'unscrewed'.

Work downstream of the blocked pipe. i.e. open up each IC or rodding eye, (small round or oval covers) until you get to the one that's NOT full of water. Rod 'upstream' towards the full IC. Once you feel the blockage clear, you'll hear the rumble of water coming from 'upstream', hint: time to bug out! Oh, and you might want to stock up on the rubber gloves first...

TOP TIP Remember that it's possible your drain access (via an IC) might be on a neighbour's property. You have the right to access them, but of course, it's polite to ask first (work together, it's probably their drain too...)

CHECK Check drains for leaks (if you suspect a problem). Similar to the hard-standing areas we looked at above, look closely at the ground over the top of any drain runs, (from a grate to an IC or between IC's for example) because when drains leak, material surrounding the pipe washes away down the drains. This erosion eventually causes visible depressions in the ground or settlement under walls and hard standing areas etc. This settlement or movement can even cause hard-standing areas to crack or break up.

Three different ways to confirm a drain problem...

Pressure test: Seal the soil & vent pipe (SVP) with a bung and place a second bung with a nipple at the lowest point in the system (usually your lowest IC. Connect a small plastic pipe to the nipple and attach a manometer and pump ball. Pump up the pressure inside the pipe to around 100mm and wait 10 mins for stabilization. After 10 mins adjust the pressure reading to 100 on the gauge. The pressure must not drop more than 25 after 5 mins. More than this means a leak.

Water test: Insert a rubber bung below the part being tested and then fill up the pipes/ICs with water (this may take some time). Top up the water after a few mins and then monitor. The level in an IC for example shouldn't drop more than a little (a little drop is normal as the water soaks into mortar/pipes/joints etc.). Significant water loss means a leak.

Visual test: hire a drain camera or make your own with a cheap endoscope connected to your laptop. Run the camera down the drain and watch the image on the screen. Look for obstruction, fats/ debris/ disposable razors/ leaves/ roots/ condoms/ sanitary items/ broken pipes/ soil/ stones/ etc. etc.

Leaking drains can also attract tree and plant roots because of the nutrient rich water. Eventually the roots will block or damage the pipe.

Repair damaged drains: You can get an idea of drain depth and direction by looking into adjacent IC's and drawing lines between them to indicate possible drain runs.

Dig down and find the pipe (this is the hardest part). Excavate around and underneath the pipe exposing the leaking section. You can also hire a drain locator to find hidden drains, making excavation more accurate.

Cut out leaking/ broken section with a suitable tool (a wood saw easily cuts plastic or a disc grinder with a stone blade for clay or concrete). Sometimes it's easier to remove a part of the pipe in the middle of the damaged section and then cut again either side of the damage, this allows the cut part to fall free and there is less chance of the blade jamming as the cut goes all the way though.

Clean up the cut ends at least 100mm (4") and chamfer the cut edge a little to tidy it up and make getting on the new joints easier. Place lubricated slip collars or rubber pipe connectors over the cut ends and insert a section of new pipe. Slide the collars/joints half and half onto the new/old pipe. Tighten any fittings if applicable.

Surround the repaired pipe with pea gravel or soft 'as dug' material. Backfill hole to the top, compacting as you go, leaving it a little high to allow the 'backfill' to settle.

Relax, you've just saved yourself thousands.....

Grinders are dangerous and easily snatch. You must have a good footing (i.e. standing firm and steady), good access to the pipe, goggles and gloves and a very steady hand are essential, (or hire someone who has experience using a grinder).

Once you're all done with the drains, scrape out/wire brush any rusty IC frame grooves and the edges of the cover. Put grease in the frame groove to make it easier to remove the covers next time. Grease any screws, if present.

MAIN STRUCTURE

MASONRY/WALLS/BRICK/BLOCK/STONE/ETC

Check for damp patches on walls (house, outbuildings, garden walls etc.).

It's important to keep masonry as dry as possible, remember that a dry wall, is a happy wall. Investigate areas that look different from the majority of the wall (darker, damp patches).

TO DO Simple ways to minimize excess moisture getting into your walls (both house and any garden walls) ...

- Repair leaking gutters or downpipes.
- Correct incorrect falls or levels on paving.
- Repair failed damp-proof courses (DPC).
- Repair damaged copings, cappings or 'drips'.
- Repair leaking roofs etc.

TOP TIP Consider replacing hard paved areas at the base of walls with small 'borders' of small stones or even soil, to lessen splash back when it rains, even as little as 15cm (6") wide will help and 30cm (12") is even better.

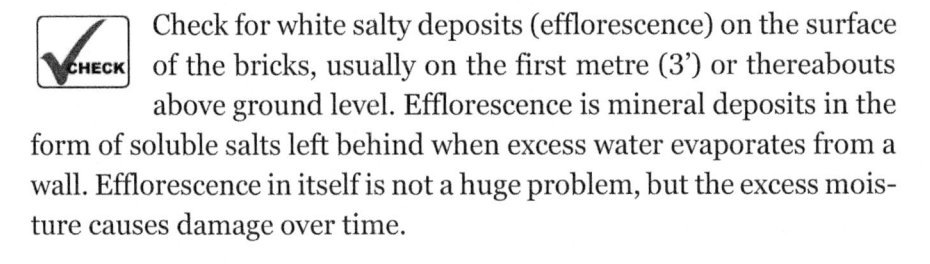

CHECK Check for white salty deposits (efflorescence) on the surface of the bricks, usually on the first metre (3') or thereabouts above ground level. Efflorescence is mineral deposits in the form of soluble salts left behind when excess water evaporates from a wall. Efflorescence in itself is not a huge problem, but the excess moisture causes damage over time.

TO DO Investigate how excess moisture is getting into the wall and remedy (check gutters, downpipes, paving falls, drains, DPC etc.). Then on a warm dry day, brush the salt away with a brush. Gentle and minimal use of water or a pressure washer can be effective, (be careful not to saturate the wall though because water in the wall is the problem don't forget). Special chemicals are also available but be careful to follow the instructions given.

CHECK Check for damaged bricks (called 'spalled' bricks). Excess moisture evaporating from the surface eventually spalls bricks, usually around the base of walls in exposed locations or damp areas. Often exacerbated by freeze/thaw cycles and/or 'too-hard' cement mortar re-pointing on older properties.

TO DO: Replace spalled bricks by chopping out the mortar around them using a plugging chisel and/or an electric SDS drill. Carefully remove the damaged brick(s) (don't damage the surrounding bricks!) and replace with a matching one.

Use a 'ready to use' lime mortar from a specialist or mix lime putty and sieved/graded sharp sand mixed 1:3 for older properties. Modern houses might use a typical mortar mix of cement, lime and soft sand mixed to a ratio of 1:1:6 + a plasticizer (chemical additive to make the mix smooth and creamy, i.e. easier to use, and slower setting).

TOP TIP: Occasionally, you may be able to turn a spalled brick around and re-use it, if the damage to the face side is minor.

TOP TIP: Occasionally, bricks spall because they are too soft for the location. Bricks below DPC level, in chimneys and in garden walls need to be tough!

Masonry painted with non-breathable paint can also suffer from spalling because of trapped moisture.

CHECK: Check for cracked bricks, especially vertical cracks running through several bricks (shear cracks). Cracked bricks indicate serious movement and require further investigation to find out what is stressing the wall, before carrying out repairs. It's possible there is foundation movement, leaking drains, tree roots etc.

TOP TIP: Monitor any cracks in brickwork (or mortar joints) to determine if movement is still 'live' and ongoing or old and stable. Buy and fix 'tell tales' across serious cracks to measure movement. Also mark the ends of a crack (with the date) to see if it travels further over time. Consider calling in a structural engineer to get their thoughts and a report for your insurance company.

TO DO: Rectify causes of live movement and allow to settle for a period before attempting to repair cracks. This might take up to a full year (i.e. all seasons).

Once cracks are stable (i.e. the movement has stopped), replace cracked bricks as per the 'replace spalled bricks' mentioned above.

CHECK: Check for cracks that zigzag down the mortar joints. Look also for seriously eroded mortar joints, i.e. more than the joint width. Shallow erosion isn't too much to worry about if there are no cracks or damp issues internally.

TO DO: Chip out the cracked mortar or clean out vulnerable eroded mortar joints to a depth of appx. twice their height (10mm or 3/8" high joints, means getting them to around 20mm or 3/4" deep). Re-point using a suitable, matching mortar as mentioned above when replacing spalled bricks.

TOP TIP: Before using new mortar on an old masonry, damp down masonry with a garden sprayer and allow to soak in a little.

Pack the new mortar joints around new bricks tightly with fairly stiff mortar, especially the top joint. Push and pack the mortar in with a finger trowel or a thin piece of wood. Full joints are important to maintain the walls strength.

Pack the joint from right to left (or left to right) to avoid pushing the mortar all the way through and off the back of the brick in single leaf masonry.

Once the mortar joint is full, tool off the front of the joint to match the surrounding brickwork. At the end of the day, gently brush the repaired areas with a soft hand brush for that extra professional finish.

CHECK: Check that any airbricks/ vents/etc. are free from debris or other obstruction (stuff stacked outside, firewood, bins etc.).

TO DO: Pull out previous attempts to block airbricks to prevent 'draughts'. Brush, vacuum or blow out debris and cobwebs etc. Move temporary obstructions.

VEGETATION

CHECK: Check any plants which are growing close to walls. Look also for any unintentional vegetation growing up or into walls.

TO DO: Annually cut any climbing plants to leave at least 30cm free space from any window, door, or roofline. Remove unintentional plants completely.

RENDERED AND PAINTED FINISHES

CHECK: Check cement rendered or painted areas for good adhesion to the wall beneath by tapping gently with your knuckles or a short stick. Hollow areas sound and feel different to the well-attached areas.

TOP TIP: Most common areas to find damage is around the base of walls, around any cracks, around windows, around leaking rainwater systems, around any metal trims embedded in the render, around anything piercing the render (screws, brackets, nails etc.), corners and edges etc.

TO DO: Investigate what's causing the failure, usually excess moisture is getting behind the surface (see above tip). Subsequent freezing 'blows' the render or paint away from the wall.

Fix the moisture problem, then cut/scrape/remove loose or flaking areas back to sound edges and replace/refinish with a matching, suitable mortar.

Sometimes walls are rendered to cover up a problem. If you have fixed the underlying problem which damaged the wall in the first place, you might not need to replace the render. However, the wall might need a breathable paint to make it look 'all-one-colour' or to 'hide' a patchwork of piecemeal repairs.

DOORS AND WINDOWS

Check paintwork to ensure the finish is still bright and intact. Especially look for flaking, splits, dullness, or other damage.

Any dull paint needs thorough preparation and re-finishing. Typically; clean, sand down to provide a key, followed by a wipe down to remove dust and an undercoat/primer. Finish with two coats of a durable top coat/finish paint. Note that you'll need paint suitable for outdoors for the outside parts.

Paint which is flaking down to bare wood needs complete removal (scrape with a metal scraper) and sand until smooth. Use a wood primer on the bare wood and then finish as normal (an undercoat plus two topcoats).

Don't use silicone sealants around painted frames because it cannot be over-painted in the future. Use a paintable caulk or mastic to fill gaps between frames and the wall.

Check for soft spots on timber frames by using your thumb. Especially at the bottom of the uprights or in the windowsill itself.

Repair any soft spots by removing them. Remove any adjacent glazing. Cut out the rotten wood and replace with good quality timber, glued, and screwed into place. Apply a primer preservative to repairs and re-finish. Re-fit glazing.

TOP TIP: It's an option to fill minor damage or soft spots with a suitable exterior grade filler designed to repair wooden frames and re-decorate as normal. Be aware this is at best a temporary repair, but if you've repaired the water ingress problem, you might get a few years out of a well filled repair (dig out as much rotten timber as you can before filling...).

CHECK: Check for leaks around glass panes, (especially on old, single glazed windows). Usually caused by missing putty or even a broken pane of glass. Make sure you're not looking at condensation which has puddled at the bottom of the glass.

TO DO: Break out and remove broken glass and scrape out old putty. Paint the glass rebate with a good primer (or shellac if you're in a hurry).

Place well-kneaded putty on the inside, vertical edge of the glass rebate and gently push new glass into it, until it's 2 or 3mm thick (1/8"). Putty the outside and smooth it to an angle with a clean knife. Re-paint once putty is firm (can take a while, days or even weeks).

TOP TIP: Repair and replace any broken glass before water ingress has a chance to rot the thin glazing bars or frame.

CHECK: Check that any plastic window frames you have are clean, especially from dust, grit, or bird droppings etc. Check the rubber seals and weather stripping for gaps or splits.

TO DO: Wash down plastic frames using regular household cleaners and wipe dry.

Wipe clean all weather seals. Replace damaged or missing seals or rubber strips.

CHECK: Check double glazed units for failed sealant. Look for hazing on the inside of the glass, inside the double-glazed unit itself.

TO DO — Fix by replacing the double-glazed unit as a whole. Sad to say, but there really is no other way of effectively repairing these at home. If you can live with the look and accept increased heat loss, there is no danger to leaving them as they are. Defogging kits and services are available, but their effectiveness and especially their longevity is questionable.

TOP TIP — Carry out repairs in warm weather, rubber seals and especially putty are both easier to work with when warm.

CHECK — Check all external sealant or caulk between door and window frames and the wall for integrity. Look for dried out, missing or split sealant.

TO DO — Scrape away damaged sealant with a scraper, being careful not to damage the frame etc. Clean down and re-apply sealant or caulk.

ROOFLINE

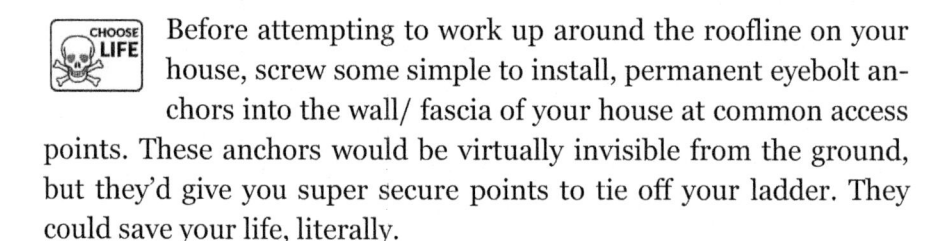

CHOOSE LIFE — Before attempting to work up around the roofline on your house, screw some simple to install, permanent eyebolt anchors into the wall/ fascia of your house at common access points. These anchors would be virtually invisible from the ground, but they'd give you super secure points to tie off your ladder. They could save your life, literally.

CHOOSE LIFE — Leaning ladders onto rainwater gutters is dangerous, period. As a minimum, secure your ladder by getting someone to stand on the bottom rung or if working alone, place a heavy bag of sand against the legs and another over the first rung and then tie the top to the above-mentioned anchor points.

GUTTERS AND DOWNPIPES

CHECK — Check the rainwater system works properly and yes, the best way to do it is when it's absolutely pouring down with rain...

TO DO — Clean any build-up of detritus out of the gutters with a brush, trowel, and bucket at least annually. After all the leaves have fallen in the autumn or fall is a good time.

CHECK — Check to make sure the rainwater is actually going into the gutter and not behind or over the front. Water 'cascading' over the front, rear or end of gutters usually means a blockage at the outlet/downpipe or a poor fall.

TO DO — Check gutters are level or fall slightly towards outlets; remove and lift up if not.

CHECK — Especially check downpipes for leaks and security. Check also that the water goes into the drain from the downpipe shoe.

TO DO — If downpipes are blocked, either flush with a running hosepipe from the top or work up from the bottom. Repair any leaking joints with new rubber seals or silicone sealant after a thorough clean.

TOP TIP — Dismantle parts that continually work themselves apart, clean and re-assemble with silicone sealant, which is a fair adhesive as well as a sealant.

FASCIA, SOFFITS, VERGES AND BARGE BOARDS

CHECK — Check condition of external woodwork such as fascia's, soffits, bargeboards, and other external wooden trims for rot, flaking paint or dull finishes.

TO DO — Cut out any rotten sections and use them as 'patterns' to mark out new repair pieces onto your new timber. Cut out the new pieces and prime/paint the new timber all round, (plus the cut ends of the existing timber). Fix the new timber into place with exterior grade nails or screws (galvanized usually). Elsewhere, scrape away any loose finishes, sand, and re-finish as necessary.

CHECK — Check condition of any vents or grills looking for any obstruction.

TO DO — Brush, vacuum or blow out debris and cobwebs etc. (nests are common here too, they're not called house sparrows for nothing!).

CHECK — Check that any insect screens behind vents are intact (tears and holes are common, mesh is pretty fragile).

TO DO — Spiders love building cobwebs in vents, so get a 'big person' to help if you're a little bit scared of spiders...

CHECK — Check condition of any bird screening, often found under the first row of profiled roofing tiles.

TO DO — Wire, cable tie or screw matching mesh over any tears or holes you find.

VERGES

CHECK — Check the verges (sloping edges of roof) for damage (missing tiles, timber missing mortar etc.), which can allow rain (and birds/insects!) in.

TO DO — Scrape out loose mortar, brush out and damp down with a garden sprayer. Re-point using a strong, stiff mortar. Mix mortar 1:3 cement to building sand (strong mix). Replace missing tiles/timber with new to match.

ROOF

TOP TIP: To examine your roof and chimney etc. closely, use a pair of binoculars or a telescope (and let the neighbours wonder…).

CHECK: Check the roof for any missing, slipped, or broken tiles, slates etc.

Look especially around the bottom, sides and top of the roof, as these are common problem areas.

TO DO: Replace tiles by pushing up the row above a little if possible. Wiggle out any broken pieces and pop the new one in. Pull down the row above. A trowel and pairs of door or wooden wedges are useful to hold up tiles slightly, especially if the surrounding tiles are nailed in place. Gloves are good.

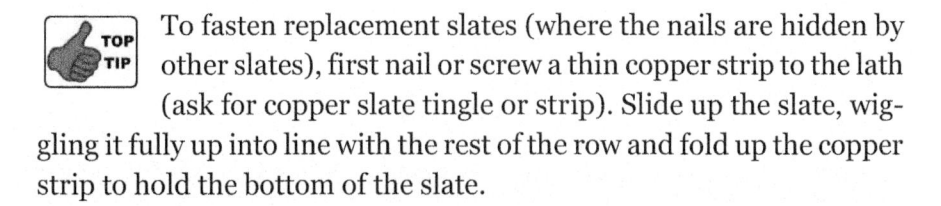

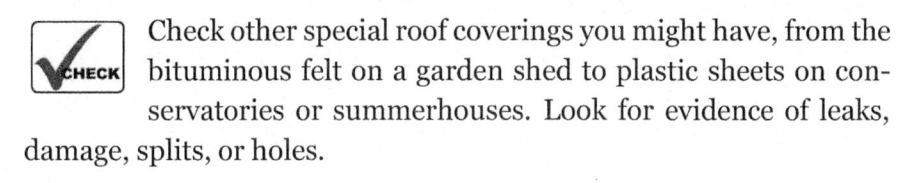

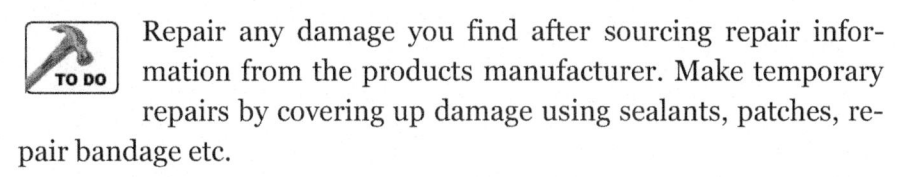

TOP TIP: To fasten replacement slates (where the nails are hidden by other slates), first nail or screw a thin copper strip to the lath (ask for copper slate tingle or strip). Slide up the slate, wiggling it fully up into line with the rest of the row and fold up the copper strip to hold the bottom of the slate.

CHECK: Check other special roof coverings you might have, from the bituminous felt on a garden shed to plastic sheets on conservatories or summerhouses. Look for evidence of leaks, damage, splits, or holes.

TO DO: Repair any damage you find after sourcing repair information from the products manufacturer. Make temporary repairs by covering up damage using sealants, patches, repair bandage etc.

TOP TIP: Always carry out an extra roof inspection after a big storm. Better to find any damage before the next one…

CHECK: Visually check ridge tiles on the rooftop for eroded or missing mortar likely to affect security. Physically check any you suspect are loose. Loose ridge tiles commonly blow off during storms..... and remember, where do you park your car.....

TOP TIP: Solid ridge tiles are probably best left in place as trying to remove them can break several tiles. Re-bed the ones that lift off easily and repoint the ones that are solid to keep a uniform look.

TO DO: Lift away loose ridge tiles. Scrape away any loose mortar and brush down. Damp down with a garden sprayer and allow to soak in. Using a fairly stiff and strong mortar, re-bed the removed ridge tiles and replace any missing mortar on the others. Trowel the mortar up to the bottom of the ridge tile following the roof profile in a smooth action pressing the mortar in firmly.

CHECK: Similarly check hip tiles running down the roof for eroded mortar and security. Hip tiles also commonly blow off during storms.

TO DO: Repairs are as above for ridge tiles. Access is usually difficult to achieve safely. Scaffolding is the only properly safe way.

TOP TIP: Mortar for bedding ridge tiles needs to be strong to withstand the weather. Try 1:3, cement to building sand mixed to a stiff consistency (not sloppy like bricklaying mortar).

CHECK: Check the condition of any flat roofed areas for signs of the covering lifting. Walk around all areas feeling for soft or spongy boards underneath your feet.

TO DO: Repairs to flat roofs are often short-lived and comparatively expensive. Complete replacement is often the best answer. Choose a reputable company with guarantees.

✅ **CHECK** Check the condition of protective UV coverings on flat roofs, such as small stones or reflective paints etc.

🔨 **TO DO** Spread out heat absorbing stones and add new to cover sparse areas. Clean and repaint reflective paints once dull or damaged.

✅ **CHECK** Check all up-stands or flashings where the roof joins other roofs or walls, for integrity.

🔨 **TO DO** Replace any displaced flashings from where they came from and re-fix using matching materials.

✅ **CHECK** Check the condition of anything that penetrates the roof covering. Such as vent pipes, dormers, Velux type 'in roof' type windows, access fixtures, fire escape equipment etc. Check especially how the item seals down onto the roof covering for damage or displacement (usually some sort of metal or rubber flashing).

🔨 **TO DO** Replace anything that's missing. Re-seat anything that's displaced or dislodged. Repair any damaged or failing flashings, seals, and rubber boots etc to maintain a watertight seal down or onto the roof covering.

👍 **TOP TIP** Remember, the best time to fix your roof is when the sun is shining....

VALLEYS

✅ **CHECK** Check any valleys between roofs for tears, splits, blockage, or damage. Metal or lead work can split if it's too thin or laid in long lengths. Joints are a good thing to allow thermal expansion and contraction.

🔨 **TO DO** Temporary repairs can be made using a variety of products such as a self-adhesive sealing strip like 'flashband' or even silicone sealant in a pinch, but replacing the damaged section is usually the only permanent solution. Lead can be welded, but this may cost more than a straightforward replacement, assuming that you can find someone who can still do it!

TOP TIP Paintwork on above roof structures (dormers etc) are often overlooked, which is a problem because their exposed location means they actually need more attention than other areas of the house.

CHIMNEY

TOP TIP Check the condition of any chimneys you have with binoculars, especially carefully check the masonry towards the top of the stack.

CHECK Check the condition of the chimney pots, look for leaning, cracks or missing parts.

TO DO Broken chimney pots need replacing with new ones, usually as part of a re-build (if the chimney pots are breaking up, the brickwork on the chimney is usually in bad shape also).

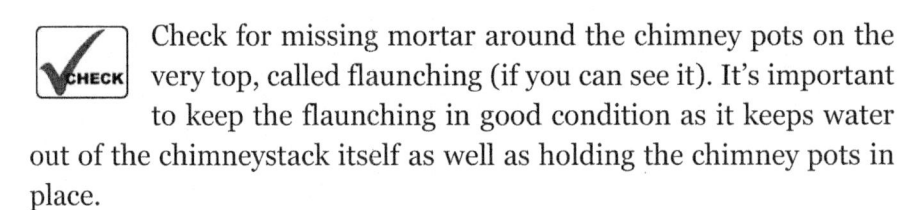

CHECK Check for missing mortar around the chimney pots on the very top, called flaunching (if you can see it). It's important to keep the flaunching in good condition as it keeps water out of the chimneystack itself as well as holding the chimney pots in place.

TO DO Remove loose mortar from around chimney pots and replace the flaunching over the whole cap using a strong mortar (1:3 cement to sharp sand mix). Ensure flaunching falls away from the pots to the outside edge of the chimney brickwork. No part of the flaunching should be less than 30-40mm thick, (preferably more) to avoid failure from frost.

TOP TIP: The chimney is the toughest place to be on your house as it's exposed to wind, rain, cold, heat and chemicals from smoke and water.

Chimneys can deteriorate to a point where it's difficult to believe they are still standing, let alone able to withstand a storm.

CHECK: Check for spalling bricks. Usually restricted to the top few courses of the chimney.

TO DO: Once the top bricks start to break up, don't mess about, have a proper scaffold erected, take down the stack brick by brick until you get to solid brickwork and then rebuild it. Gaining access to chimneys is difficult and expensive, but never attempt work on a chimney without a proper scaffolding. Never work on a chimney from a ladder...ever. Seriously, I really mean it! (I stupidly, naively did it as a young guy and it sucks...)

CHECK: Check for eroded mortar joints. The depth of an eroded mortar joint shouldn't exceed the joints height. Generally, this might mean they need re-pointing once they are more than 12mm (½") deep.

TO DO: Re-point any seriously eroded mortar joints with a matching mortar. 1:3 lime putty to sieved sharp sand works well on older buildings. 1:4 cement to soft building sand for modern buildings (after around 1930 or so, depending where you are). The mortar is a little stronger for chimneys (compared to regular walls) due to their severe exposure to weather.

As with the walls above, damp down the masonry with a garden sprayer and allow to soak in a little. Pack the mortar joints tightly with fairly stiff mortar. Once the mortar joint is full, tool off the front of the joint to match the surrounding brickwork. At the end of the day, gently brush the repaired areas with a soft hand brush for that extra professional finish.

CHECK Check any flashings you have are in place, tight to the wall and well secured into the mortar joints.

TO DO Push displaced flashings back into place, secure with clips (if applicable) and reseal with mortar or a special sealant for the material.

CHOOSE LIFE Again, never attempt to closely inspect or work on a chimney unless you have a good head for heights, duh!

TV EQUIPMENT

CHECK Check aerials, satellite dish etc for security of their mountings and fasteners. Corrosion is often a problem.

TO DO Paint any rusty parts after wire brushing loose rust away. Rust stabilising paints such as Hammerite are good for this. To be honest though, it's probably easier, cheaper, and quicker to just replace badly rusted mountings.

INDOORS

BASEMENTS

CHECK Check how your basement smells (if applicable of course), during your first few seconds down there, (breath out as you walk down, and then take a good sniff!). How does it smell right then? Your brain will filter out the smell after a few minutes, but that does not mean it has 'gone away'...

Look (and feel) for damp patches or cracks in the walls or floor, especially on walls which face outside (i.e. have soil against them).

Look for tell-tale white stains indicating dried out patches, salts (efflorescence) on the walls or loose material/paint etc.

TOP TIP Damp in basements is one of the most misdiagnosed problems you'll ever see. Proper 'rising damp' is remarkably uncommon (but possible of course). More often than not it's typically caused by...

- Condensation, (warm air meeting cold surfaces), caused by cold basements with not enough ventilation.
- External surface problems, runoff (water from the roof or yard) finding its way into the walls.
- Raised natural, ground water levels (high rainfall, flooding etc.).

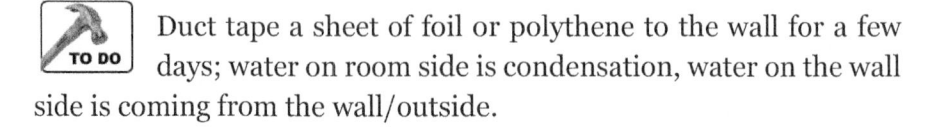

TO DO Duct tape a sheet of foil or polythene to the wall for a few days; water on room side is condensation, water on the wall side is coming from the wall/outside.

TO DO Check the basement regularly and keep a log of when the damp is worse. Note the weather conditions or anything else you think might be a factor.

See the outdoors section above and do as much as you can to keep water from getting into the wall from outside. Be aware it may take a long time for any external improvements you make to affect internal dampness. The ground and solid walls can hold a lot of water when saturated. Saturated stuff like this takes a very long time to dry out, many months even. After removing the source of the water ingress, improving heating and ventilation along with a de-humidifier will help to speed up the drying out process.

If there is naturally occurring ground water around your house, then Google, "basement waterproofing" to learn more about waterproofing options open to you. No solution is cheap or simple though and many are arguably specialised jobs best left to good contractors.

FLOORING

CHECK Check all flooring for anything new or unusual and pay particular attention around exterior doors, around shower trays, sinks, toilets etc plus around refrigerators, washing machines and dishwashers etc.

Look for localised discolouration, damage, or different feeling areas of any kind. Investigate further anything you find straight away and remember that water can run a long way from the source of the problem.

TO DO Lift up or remove any floor coverings. At this point, light water damage may dry out without causing any damage to the subfloor, (depending upon what it's made from, concrete for example, tolerates water easily, but chipboard does not).

If the subfloor is soft, spongy, or otherwise damaged, remove it as necessary. Repairs to the floors supports might be required if the water leak went on for some time (leaking bathtub or shower sealant being a classic). Cut out damaged material until you reach good material. Timber joists usually need replacing in their entirety.

Once the floor is 'open', allow plenty of time for any moisture to dry out before replacing floor coverings, lest you unintentionally seal in any moisture.

Specialists are usually required to insert 'spot' repairs on most floor coverings (stitching in carpet; welding in vinyl, etc.) and the cost may approach outright replacement of the whole covering (replacement is often quicker than repairs).

TOP TIP Don't forget to repair causes of damage to floors first, (leaking shower doors, leaking bathroom sealant, dodgy dishwasher etc. etc.).

WALLS

CHECK Check for cracks and monitor them over time, noting any changes.

TO DO Seasonal movement is difficult to 'cure'. Use flexible fillers or decorators caulk along with lining paper before re-painting.

Some cracks at drywall junctions re-open each year. You could consider pulling out the old corner tape. Then find and remove the fasteners in the corner, followed by re-taping and filling the joint. This creates a 'floating' corner that 'might' resist the movement causing the cracking. It's a somewhat experimental solution though! Google "truss uplift" to learn more about this method.

CHECK Check for discolouration or spoiling of finishes, especially around windows or next to external doorways. Check high up near the ceiling level, especially if there are bathrooms, kitchens, utility rooms or roofs above. Check for dents, holes, and poor paint finishes.

TO DO Fix any condensation issues which might be causing damage and then re-decorate as required. Plus, wipe paintwork clean annually, especially around light fittings that become dirty from hands and fingers etc.

CEILINGS

CHECK Pretty much as above for walls with the addition of checking for sagging of older ceilings (might indicate that plaster has separated from the wooden lath).

TO DO Repair damage as above for walls. Plus, wipe paintwork clean annually, especially around light fittings that attract dust (btw. they all do!).

TOP TIP Keep an eye on granddad too, years of his farts and stinking pipe will play havoc on the paintwork on the ceiling in the library or den...

WINDOWS

CHECK Check paint condition for dullness, flaking etc at least annually (every two years at most) especially in exposed areas.

TO DO — Thoroughly prepare and re-decorate any poor finishes as required, similar to the work involved in painting the exterior of the window only using paints for indoor use.

CHECK — Check that hinges, stays, handles and locks are free and operate properly.

TO DO — Wipe dust and debris from hinges and stays. Sparingly drip lubricant on all moving parts, wiping away any excess with a lint free cloth or tissue paper in a pinch.

TOP TIP — Petroleum jelly (Vaseline), WD40 (based on fish oils), light machine oil and regular grease (lithium) etc. are good lubricants but they do attract dust. Consider instead a dry type lube.

TOP TIP — Clean away and reapply often in dusty areas (and consider changing to a 'dry' lubricant).

CHECK — Check for condensation which will cause problems on some older windows causing the timber to go rotten or mouldy.

TO DO — Lessen condensation by improving ventilation and raising the average room temperature. In severe cases, you might have to leave the curtains or blinds open a little to allow the rooms heat to warm up the window past the 'dew' point. Avoid activities that increase humidity (drying wet clothes indoors etc.) and ensure your kitchen/bathroom extract fans operate properly, preferably with humidity sensors or timers which stay on after use.

TOP TIP — Check that cold air is not penetrating the external sealant around the window. Fill any gaps you find with a suitable frame sealant.

CHECK — Check self-adhesive draught-proofing strips for gaps or displacement.

TO DO — Carefully cut and remove damaged or displaced sections and stick new pieces of draught-proofing strip into place. If you have push in style strips, pull out damaged parts, snip them off. Measure and cut new strips of draught excluder and push them back into the narrow slot with your fingers (or a blunt instrument such as a paint scraper, if tight).

CHECK — Check brush type draught excluder strips for debris (and check the fit for any gaps too).

TO DO — Clean around the inside parts of the window with a vacuum or brush to remove any build-up of debris from the brush strips.

DOORS

CHECK — Check for loose hinges (listen and feel for movement when you open/close the door).

TO DO — Poke out the paint from screw heads and check that the hinge screws are tight. Remove any screws that won't tighten up and dip a matchstick (or cocktail stick or thin sliver of wood) into wood glue and pop it back into the empty hole and snap it off flush. Replace the screw and tighten. There's usually no need to wait for the glue to dry.

CHECK — Check for tight or uneven gaps between the door and frame that are allowing binding or catching. Most doors need 2 or 3mm all around for good operation.

TO DO — If you have tight spots, adjust the doors fit if possible. Hinges can be recessed further into the frame (or door) by using a sharp chisel to deepen slightly the hinge rebate. Conversely you can pack hinges out with cardboard shims before tightening up the screws.

If the door has swelled and is catching, plane down the tight spot where the door catches the frame until it clears by 1 or 2mm.

If the frame was poorly fitted or has moved, remove the screws fastening it to the wall and adjust the packing shims to straighten the frame. If there is no gap/shims, then plane the door to suit the frame and refinish the paint.

CHECK Check for worn/missing paint or finishes on the doors edges (plus if you've planed anything down to fit properly).

TO DO Refinish any bare areas (sandpaper, prime/undercoat, and top coats).

CHECK Check operation of hinges, locks, and handles. Look for stiffness in operation or loose/slack parts.

TO DO Lubricate hinges, locks, handles, and other hardware annually (see windows tip for lube). Tighten loose fasteners and replace any worn out components.

CHECK Check that draught proofing is in place. Don't forget the letterbox if you have one. Check for drafts using the back of a damp hand or a smoking incense stick.

TO DO Fill any gaps with draught-proofing strips. Remove damaged or displaced sections and stick new sections in place. Vacuum clean brush type strips.

KITCHEN AND OR UTILITY AREAS

CABINETS/DOORS

CHECK Check cabinet doors and drawers for alignment to make sure doors or drawers re not catching each other. Listen/feel also for movement or 'clonking' in the hinges etc.

TO DO — Make sure hinge back plates are tight to the cabinet first, and then adjust hinges until the gaps between doors or drawers are even. Drawers often have adjusters on the side.

KITCHEN SINK

CHECK — Check the seal between the kitchen sink and the work surface is intact. Especially at the rear of the sink where it gets wet most. Look for lifting of the work surface and or signs of damp underneath (yes you will have to empty all the junk out of the cupboard!

TO DO — The best way to repair this is to remove the sink completely and reapply clear silicone sealant to it and re-set the sink. However, this can be difficult if some of the original sealant is holding firm (one of the ironies of life, half fails and half is like concrete).

An intermediate repair is to scrape away the failed areas of sealant, clean thoroughly and re-apply new silicone sealant around the outer edge of the sink, smoothed over with a damp finger.

CHECK — Check the trap or 'U' bends under the sink. This one has a lot to deal with on a daily basis from bits of food to grease and fat. See 'Traps in General' in the Plumbing Section in a little while.

TOP TIP — Your grandmother knows best when it comes to sink maintenance. Always wipe away splashed water from around the sink straight away. Never, *ever* let water sit on work surfaces around the kitchen sink. Avoid leaving a damp dishcloth on the sink edge too.

indoors

COOKER HOOD/EXTRACT

[CHECK] Check any removable filters or screens for grease build-up (this is why you need to save the instructions!).

[TO DO] Replace any clogged carbon type filters with new ones. Washable screens are usually okay to go in the dishwasher.

[CHECK] Whilst you have the screens out, check inside. If you've been a bit lax in cleaning the filters you might find a build-up of grease, depending on your, erm, how can I put it politely, hmm, let's say 'cooking style'... (i.e. if you fry everything...). Grease can lead to nasty smells if left.

[TO DO] Unplug or isolate the fan/unit first. Put something onto the hob before you start to minimise the clean up afterwards. Use a good degreasing cleaner and plenty of kitchen paper or old rags. Be careful not to spray cleaner onto electrical parts.

REFRIGERATOR

[CHECK] Check your refrigerator's interior drain, because it easily clogs and can even freeze up.

[TO DO] In many refrigerators the internal drain is right at the back near the bottom and may or may not have a little plastic 'filter/bung' which lifts out for cleaning. Find the drain and clean out any debris plus any ice. Don't use a knife etc to lever out ice, because the plastic may be thin and brittle. Use a hairdryer for a minute or two on a warm setting and try again by hand/cloth.

[CHECK] On freestanding refrigerators check the cooling fins (the large black wire mesh radiator covering most of the rear) for dust at least annually.

home maintenance checklist

TO DO — Pull the refrigerator out to gain access to the rear (watch the electrical cable and plug, you might need to temporarily unplug it). Using the little brush attachment and your vacuum cleaner, remove any dust from the radiator grid to improve efficiency.

CHECK — Check the magnetic seal around the door looking for debris, damage, splits etc. Leaks around the seal can cause the refrigerator to work extra hard to maintain cooling, using more electricity and wearing out motors etc.

TO DO — Clean away any grime or debris. Replace any damaged seals or any which don't maintain a good airtight seal to the refrigerator cabinet (they can become compressed over time).

CHECK — Check also that the refrigerator is sitting level. Wobbly refrigerators can struggle to maintain a good door seal, leading to inefficiency problems and overwork.

TO DO — Adjust the screw in/out feet on the front or rear of the refrigerator to level it up. Some models have special adjusters (especially for rear feet) accessible through holes in the plastic front; turn these with a screwdriver, usually clockwise to go up and anti-clockwise for, yup you guessed it, to go down.

CHECK — Check any ventilation grills or vents for obstruction (on the top at the back and on the bottom at the front usually). Especially if you store stuff on the top of your refrigerator.

TO DO — Make sure stuff hasn't migrated back and covered the refrigerators ventilation areas because this will increase electricity consumption as the refrigerator struggles to keep cool with a restricted fresh air flow.

TOP TIP — Clean up refrigerator spills as they happen. Keeping sauce bottles etc clean helps... At least annually, completely empty the refrigerator into coolers. Remove all shelves etc, wash with mild dishwashing soap and dry them. Clean inside the refrigerator using a couple of teaspoons of baking or bicarbonate of soda in a litre of water. A toothbrush is great for getting into corners. Allow to dry before putting everything back, minus the old stuff that needs throwing away!

WASHING MACHINE

Check your washing machines water hoses for damage such as bulges, perishing or surface splits by removing them. Check also for tired or worn out sealing washers.

Turn off the water isolating valve first (most washing machines have one where the hose attaches. If not turn of the main water supply).

Remove the water hoses by carefully unscrewing both ends. Most hose ends have 'ears' and are only 'hand tight'. If they have been left for a long time you might need 'help' to undo them; try a pair of cloth covered grips/wrench. With the water hoses off, flex them one way and then the other looking for the aforementioned bulges, perishing or surface splits.

Hook out the washers in each end. Deeply grooved, hard or overly compressed washers are vulnerable and may soon leak. Replace the washers (or at least turn them over so a 'fresh' face is on the sealing side). Make sure they seat properly, below the threads and over the little raised centre section.

The water pipes will likely be full of, yup, you guessed it, water. Either hold both ends of the pipe high and then tip the water out into a bucket, or, undo one end and lower it to a bowl on the ground and let it drain.

Check the washing machines wastewater pipe for damage and make sure it's held securely.

TO DO — Tighten any loose fasteners/clips etc. and add cable ties to hold the pipe in place if applicable.

TOP TIP — Consider replacing the hoses/washers if they are more than 10 years old or so, regardless of the results of a visual inspection. It's likely the hoses will be stiff and hard after this time and washers compressed.

CHECK — Check that the washing machine is still level and in place from time to time. Washing machines vibrate....a lot!

TO DO — Adjust the screw up/down feet until level. Tighten any locking nuts up to the machine, once the feet are adjusted (hold the foot as you tighten the lock nut, or you risk moving it).

CHECK — Check the washing machines soap dispensers. They usually build up quite a bit of old powder and fabric softeners.

TO DO — Read the machines instructions and remove the drawer. Soak the drawer in hot water for a few minutes and then scrub with a washing up brush. Dry and replace.

TUMBLE DRYERS (REALLY, YOU'RE STILL USING ONE?)

CHECK — Check all lint filters; there may be more than one (back to those instructions you saved again!).

CHECK — Check water reservoirs on condensing dryers (you know what I'm going to say don't you...?).

TO DO — Clean lint filters (and empty water reservoirs) before using, every time. On condensing machines, occasionally remove the condenser (bottom behind panel usually) and rinse away any dust and lint down there as well (your shower works well for this). Wipe down rubber seals and re-fit the dry condenser.

A build-up of lint is a common cause of house fires as lint builds up at an incredible rate if unchecked.

BATHROOM

DAMP

Check for water damage everywhere. The bathroom is the No.1 place to suffer from damage caused by damp (obviously!). Damage shows up as discolouration or swellings, lumps, bumps, or bubbles depending on the material affected.

Rectify source of water ingress first. Possible causes could be condensation (increase heating and ventilation), a leaking pipe or faulty appliance/fitting or bad sealants (replace). Remove damaged material until you're back to sound stuff and replace as necessary.

Leave trickle vents open in bathrooms to allow condensation from drying towels to escape.

SILICONE SEALANT

Check silicone sealant seals. Usually present between differing materials and/or changes of direction, classic ones are:-

- Bathtub to ceramic tile or water resistant 'aqua' panels.
- Sinks to ceramic tile or water resistant 'aqua' panels.
- Shower panels or frames to ceramic tile or water resistant 'aqua' panels.
- Vertical and horizontal joints in between tiles or water resistant 'aqua' panels (corners and floor to wall).
- Toilet to floor.

You may also have:-

- Ceramic tile to timber (even if this makes the timber difficult to paint in the future). There are paintable sealants and caulks out there.
- Ceramic tile to window, plastic/metal, or wood, (see above).
- Glass to glass or mirror to mirror.
- Metal to glass.

CHECK Check for splits in the sealant, often caused by seasonal movement of the house, poor support of heavy items (like the bath) or simply old, ineffective, or poor-quality silicone.

TOP TIP If your bathtub silicone keeps splitting, remove the bath panel and check that the bathtub is properly supported. Each leg should be tight down to the floor. Check that legs are positioned close to a floor joist or on a timber spreader. Legs sitting on floorboards only (e.g. in between floor joists) can flex under a full load. Wind them up (one at a time) and slip a hefty lump of timber under them, if possible. 50mm x 100 or 150mm (2"x 4" or 6"), long enough to span two joists is good. Then wind the leg back down onto the spreader.

CHECK Check for black mould which could be a sign of poor ventilation/lack of heating/standing water etc.

CHECK Check for loss of adhesion between the sealant and the substrate.

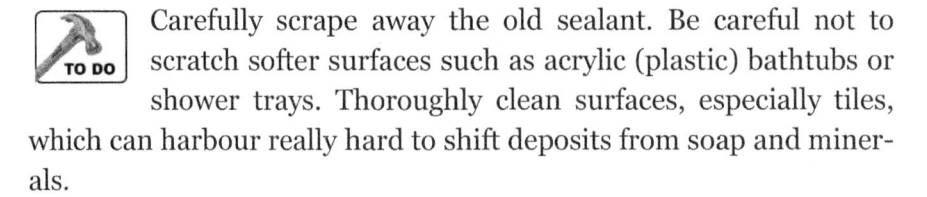

TO DO Carefully scrape away the old sealant. Be careful not to scratch softer surfaces such as acrylic (plastic) bathtubs or shower trays. Thoroughly clean surfaces, especially tiles, which can harbour really hard to shift deposits from soap and minerals.

Apply an even bead of silicone and use a silicone smoothing tool which have a small rubber blade. These work well as they remove excess silicone from both surfaces as you slowly draw them over the wet silicone. Or in many cases, a dampened finger works just fine.

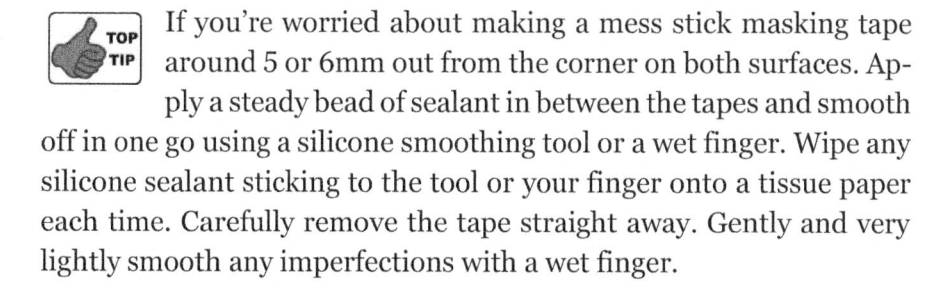

TOP TIP If you're worried about making a mess stick masking tape around 5 or 6mm out from the corner on both surfaces. Apply a steady bead of sealant in between the tapes and smooth off in one go using a silicone smoothing tool or a wet finger. Wipe any silicone sealant sticking to the tool or your finger onto a tissue paper each time. Carefully remove the tape straight away. Gently and very lightly smooth any imperfections with a wet finger.

TOP TIP Practice your silicone skills on the inside corners of a cardboard box first. (don't laugh, it's tricky to do well and silicone is cheap).

TOP TIP Avoid cheap silicone sealant because it doesn't last very long. Look for silicone from well-known brands that contain mould inhibitors designed for sanitary ware.

TOP TIP As mentioned above, try to avoid using silicone up to painted surfaces, as it cannot be over-painted (looks great right up the point where you needing to decorate again though...).

MOULD

CHECK Check for black spots of mould everywhere, but particularly next to outside walls where cold air from outside hitting the top of any exposed areas of the ceiling causes damp air to condense on the underneath of the ceiling. Condensation leads to mould.

TO DO In the loft/attic, ensure the insulation goes right up to the edge of the ceiling and preferably, goes over the Wallplate and joins up with insulation from the outside wall, to create an insulated 'envelope' with no gaps where cold air can strike the back of the ceiling.

But. It's very important that the insulation doesn't block any ventilation gaps which allow air to flow into and out of the loft or attic space (cold roofs only). Plastic spacers are available which slip under the roof covering and on top of the insulation to ensure that air can flow freely into and out of the cold loft space.

EXTRACT FANS

Check bathroom extract fan for efficiency to prevent damaging build-up of damp air during showers or drying clothes etc.

Switch the fan on and hold a sheet of paper up to the fan, it should snap onto the vent and stay in place by suction alone (remove the paper after a second or two). Clean dust from any vents and the fan blades, if at all possible. A vacuum cleaner and the brush attachment works well. (See Fan Ducting in the Loft or Attic section later...).

Consider wiring the fan into the light circuit so that the fan comes on with the lamp and you can't 'forget' to turn it on. Or consider a better fan with a humidity sensor or a timer and give it its own power supply...

PLUMBING

TAPS AND FAUCETS

Check taps or faucets for drips. Also check for ease of use, i.e. stiff or tight levers etc. which can be a sign of mineral deposits building up on components or hardening of any rubber seals.

TOP TIP: Before dismantling anything, don't forget to put the plug into the plughole, so you don't lose any small parts down the drain...

TO DO: The four main types or tap/faucet are compression (old-fashioned rubber washer) plus three 'washerless' types, ball, disc, and cartridge. Repair kits or spare parts are available for all types.

Service dripping, tight or stiff taps by dismantling and replacing worn components. First, switch off the water (duh!). Find the 'hidden' or small screw that holds the handle in place (sometimes under a small plastic cover on the top etc.). Remove all components and lay them out in logical order from left to right on a tea towel. Clean everything and lubricate rubber parts with plumber's silicone grease. Re-assemble in reverse order. If that doesn't work, then you'll need a suitable repair kit to replace worn parts.

Some rubber parts can be lubricated and turned around to last a little longer, but most parts are so cheap, (especially the older type of rubber compression washers) that re-using them is a false economy.

TOP TIP: Dismantle your tap/faucet and take the internal parts to your merchant for advice and replacement parts (this works well for many things!).

WATER TRAPS (IN GENERAL)

CHECK: It's the same procedure that we looked at above for the kitchen sink...

Pop an old towel underneath first to catch spills. Gently unscrew the bottom of the trap (bottle type) or unscrew compression retaining collars (P, U or S pipe bends). Carefully remove the trap parts keeping them level and tip any water into a bucket (or the sink above, if the plug holds a good seal).

Wash all parts thoroughly in hot soapy water. Make sure any washers or seals are in good condition. Reassemble and screw up hand tight (i.e. don't go crazy; a slightly compressed seal is the aim), overtightening can easily distort the seals, causing leaks. Run some water into the trap and check for leaks before removing the towel.

TOP TIP: Don't forget to check and re-tighten any removed traps or pipes after a few days, as pouring hot water etc. into a trap often causes newly tightened plastic fittings to loosen.

WASTE PIPES

CHECK: Check for problems with noise and/or slow draining which can mean there's an obstruction in the pipe going to the main drain.

TOP TIP: Check for blockages in the trap under the sink first. Which also gives you access to the pipework if there are no other access points. See 'Traps in General' mentioned above.

TO DO: First thing to try is the old fashioned but effective, sink plunger. Block off any overflow holes with a suitably sized cork, screwed up rubber glove, cloth, a piece of duct tape or your thumb etc.

Place the plunger over the plughole and pump up and down. Run a little water into the sink as well to get things moving. Plunging pulls the water up and down the pipe rapidly and usually clears obstructions quite impressively.

For more serious blockages, use a cheap plumber's drain clearing tool. This is a long flexible spring that you insert into the pipe and wind around and around, up, and down to physically clear away blockages.

TOP TIP: Waste pipes can also be cleaned using store bought drain cleaning chemicals. Homemade recipes also exist online to make your own cleaning chemicals using baking powder and vinegar or soda crystals and boiling water etc. Your mileage may vary though.... And they definitely won't clear serious physical blockages.

BOILERS/HEATERS/AIR CONDITIONING

Check any vents and that everything works properly. Get any gas heating systems inspected by a heating engineer annually. Peace of mind for less than a day's wages and much cheaper than a funeral...

Having your boiler/ heating/ cooling system serviced annually is cheaper and safer than calling an engineer when there is an emergency. Plus, being a regular client with your local plumbing and heating engineer might also mean you'll get better service for those other little jobs you need help with.

Apart from following the maintenance instructions which come with the appliance, there is not too much you can do yourself on some of these systems. In fact some countries have strict laws in place to stop you working on certain appliances (gas units for example in the UK).

Check your carbon monoxide detectors (you do have one, right?) if you're burning any kind of fuel (gas, oil etc.) because faulty appliances which don't completely burn the fuel properly, risk producing poisonous carbon dioxide gas, which is colourless, odourless, and deadly.

Clean all vents and grills to ensure good airflow. Vacuum cleaners and a soft paintbrush are good for this.

Remove any obstructions from around vents to ensure good airflow around the whole unit (such as boxes, coats, stored goods etc).

Book your annual inspection with a local friendly heating engineer!

OVERFLOWS

[CHECK] Check overflow pipes from water cisterns/systems etc. which stick out from your outside walls, (or roof line) for drips or leaks. They should be dry.

[TO DO] Investigate any drips, starting at the other end of the pipe inside the house (bathroom or loft/attic usually) to find out why the water level is creeping up past normal levels.

Anything which controls a water level will have a float and a shutoff valve. Valves have sealing washers which compress and harden over time. Debris can also allow a little water to creep past a seal. Replace worn washers on shut off valves or replace the whole valve. Check also that the float has not filled with water and adjust it to correct the water level. Simple systems require bending the arm holding the float to adjust the level. Others have a movable arm holding the float.

EXTERNAL TAPS AND PIPES.

[CHECK] Obviously when the temperature falls below 0°C (32°F), water freezes so check that all pipes and taps which live outside have a means of draining and isolation (isolating valves inside the house and a drain cock at the lowest point outside).

[TOP TIP] Don't forget frozen pipes burst and leak when they thaw, not when they freeze!

[TO DO] Turn off the valve and then open up the drain cock and leave open (because some valves weep a little over time). Remember to do this *before* the weather turns cold enough to freeze water!

[TOP TIP] If you just have a tap on an outside wall with no visible pipework, insulated winter covers are available which prevent the water from freezing.

indoors

ELECTRICAL SYSTEM

SAFETY TRIP SWITCH

CHECK — Check your consumer unit (fuse board) and learn how the 'test switch' works if so equipped.

Follow the instructions printed next to the test switch. Usually you just press the button and this 'trips' the whole power to the house. Re-set by lifting the main breaker switch.

CHOOSE LIFE — Ensure all your breakers/fuses are correctly labelled so you can isolate parts of the electrical system should you need to carry out inspections or repairs. Check that each breaker/fuse actually kills the power to that area by double checking that the lights/appliances go off on activation of the breaker or removing the fuse.

TOP TIP — Remember to keep a torch on, or very close to your consumer unit in a place you can find in total darkness. I like magnetic ones which you can stick to the box itself.

SWITCHES AND POWER OUTLETS

CHECK — Check each switch and power outlet for correct operation, security (to the wall) and integrity (i.e. not cracked or broken). You can buy a tester which you just plug in and it checks each wire for faults.

CHOOSE LIFE — Make sure that those new appliances added over the years don't lead to permanent extension leads or multi way plug adapters which may overload an outlet and are a common cause of house fires.

Consider hiring an electrician to add power sockets in areas with lots of appliances, such as behind entertainment centres or in the kitchen.

Replace any non-functioning, cracked or broken switch or power outlets with good quality new ones from a recognized brand. Try to avoid the cheap ones, they are often not very durable.

APPLIANCES

Check also your electrical appliances and other electrical items. Examine leads and plugs, looking for splits, stray wires, or any other damage.

Check that the outer insulation is secure in the plug and the coloured inner cores are not visible. Replace any damaged cable immediately.

Unscrew the cover from plugs with visible inner cores and loosen the cable clamp, push the outer insulation through the cable clamp and re-tighten. Replace the plug cover, being careful not to trap the inner cores.

Many fires are started by appliances and their power cords rather than the house electrical system or wiring itself (TVs, washing machines, tumble dryers, dishwashers, microwave and conventional ovens, toasters etc.). Check cables, plugs, vents and follow the manufacturers safety instructions. It's good advice to *not* run these things whilst you're out of the house too, just in case...

LOFT OR ATTIC

WATER LEAKS

Check for water stains on roof members, running down brickwork on gable ends and chimneys. Often seen as dried out whitish areas. Obviously checking after it has been raining for a few hours might enable you to see leaks as they happen. Look for dark patches and feel them to confirm it's wet if possible.

TO DO — On the next dry day, inspect the roof above the area where you suspect the leak and remedy any defects you find (missing/broken tiles, poor flashings etc). Be warned that water can 'travel' along roof timbers inside and leak some distance away from the actual problem with the roof covering.

TOP TIP — If your attic doesn't have floorboards, wear boots or sturdy footwear to increase your stability when stepping from joist to joist.

TOP TIP — As a minimum, consider building 'rat runs' from old planks or floorboards, screwed to the ceiling joists to give you safe and accident free access to areas you might need to get too in an emergency (like a water tank etc.).

INSULATION

CHECK — Loft/attic spaces are gradually filling up with insulation as regulations add a little depth each time they are updated. Check that you have a good depth over the whole area. An absolute minimum of 150mm (6") helps prevent some heat loss, but 250mm or more is better.

TOP TIP — Since 2003, the current recommended minimum depth in the UK is 270mm (almost 11"). More is expected soon...

TO DO — If the original insulation is in good shape (not compressed or full of dust and debris) you can add new insulation on top of it. Really old insulation is likely to be fairly ineffective and should be removed before adding new insulation.

Fiberglass insulation was invented by the very devil himself and supplied direct from his workshops in hell. It's truly awful stuff to work with. You must avoid at all costs breathing in the dust which emanates from it like the foul, sulphurous stink of the devil. Only kidding, well, only about the devil stuff. Fiberglass is still horrible, and you'll need protective gear like masks, goggles, and gloves as a minimum. Expect to itch even after the shower. In fact, rinse away the fibres with the shower on cool to start with, because hot water opens up your pores and increases the problem.

If you have/want floorboards on your top floor, first ensure the fibreglass is level with the top of your ceiling joists, then use dense, rigid underfloor type polystyrene on top of the ceiling joists before placing the floorboards on top glued together at the joints (floating floor). Alternatively raise the depth of the ceiling joists by adding timber to their tops (or perpendicular to them) before filling with fibreglass again and boarding the top (fixed floor).

TOP TIP Incidentally, related to insulation is draughts. If you can feel cold air coming in from unusual places, i.e. around skirting boards, electrical sockets, pipes, vents, attic hatches etc. then it means there is unintentional gaps in the insulation. Remove the item if possible and push fiberglass into any small gaps you find.

TOP TIP Most people forget to insulate the loft or attic hatch on cold roofs. Fit a piece of polystyrene (or two!) to the back of the loft hatch using double-sided tape or a polystyrene safe adhesive.

Don't forget to add a compressible weather-strip seal to the edge where the hatch sits to make it airtight and stop warm air from getting into the cold attic space and causing condensation.

WATER TANKS

CHECK In cold attics, check any water tanks (plus the pipes that feed them) to ensure they are well wrapped with insulation to protect against freezing.

TO DO Juggle any slipped insulation back into place and secure using duct tape or string. Usually there is no insulation directly underneath water tanks (to allow a little heat to keep the water from freezing). Instead take the insulation up the sides and over the top of any tank (make the top easy to remove however, for future maintenance).

Old metal water or central heating tanks need checking for leaks or weeping due to corrosion. Consider replacing any old metal tanks as soon as possible because it's a case of when, rather than if, they will leak.

Ensure any overflow pipes are actually connected, in the right place and properly supported to provide a fall to the outside.

VENTILATION

CHECK Check for vents, at eaves level (strips or circles of mesh), in gable end walls (airbricks) and at ridge level (ridge tile vents) plus any vents you see in the roof covering (tile vents).

TO DO Move any loft insulation that's blocking any ventilation gaps or systems. Clear debris/etc from any partially blocked screens, airbricks, vents, or mesh etc by gently brushing, using a vacuum cleaner, or blowing them through with compressed air if you have a compressor. Also, see 'roofline' above, some of these vents are easier to access from outside.

TOP TIP All roofs need ventilation to minimise damp problems caused by warm air rising from living spaces and condensing on cold roof coverings.

FAN DUCTING

CHECK Check that any ducting for fans (bathroom, kitchen etc) is in its proper place and there is no air escaping into the space.

Inspect joints for air tightness and refasten or re-tape any loose ones. (use regular duct tape, the key is in the name...). Leaking ducts can cause condensation problems when the warm air escapes and condenses on the cold underside of the roof.

UNWANTED CREATURES

WOODWORM

CHECK — Look for small holes in timber and especially for 'frass' (insect droppings) which can look like sawdust, as this may mean you have wood worm or other wood eating insects.

TO DO — Depending on the severity of the evidence, you might consider calling in pest control experts, as dealing with woodworm can involve some pretty nasty chemicals.

Otherwise, deal with small infestations by soaking the affected timber with a proprietary woodworm killing chemical. Always follow the instructions when using pesticides, especially regarding what to wear when applying it (usually, a mask, goggles, and gloves as a minimum).

BEES AND WASPS

CHECK — Check for nests. There are many different types of nest builders out there, so track the insects when you see them, follow them 'home' etc.

TO DO — Fill in any holes you see insects flying into (unless they are a friendly type and then you should wait for the cold weather). Try to remove food sources, i.e. manage your waste/rubbish/garbage properly inside and outside your home (keep covered etc.).

Remove aggressive wasps hanging type nests by spraying with an approved insecticide in the dark, (when they are more docile), being careful to wear a mask and protective clothing.

For the very brave, I've seen many nests removed in the dark using no more than a thick plastic bag. Approach the nest quietly in the dark and quickly slide the open bag up and over the whole nest, (preferably without touching the nest itself) and grasp the thin 'stalk' at the top to break it free. Working quickly tie a knot in the top of the bag or slide the zip-lock. Place the nest in a container with a tight-fitting lid (anything from an old saucepan to a metal dustbin). Leave for a few days and the wasps should perish.

Friendly bees, such as honey bees etc. should be collected by local enthusiasts. Your local authority will have the telephone numbers of people to help you. Do not kill off friendly bees!

Bees and wasps are important pollinators and are seriously under threat. If you fill any active holes in your home, it's only fair and decent to provide somewhere else for them to nest. Create a quiet place full of holes for them to explore and hope that they like it enough to move into. Google your insects to find out what habitats they like and don't like. Orientation and sun play an important part for most insects.

RODENTS (CUTE OR HORRORS? UP TO YOU!)

Check for evidence (nests, droppings, gnawing, tracks, etc) that might mean that you have non-paying 'tenants' in your home; *birds, squirrels, mice, or even rats* are common.

Try to find their access holes. Sprinkle flour or talcum powder around areas you suspect and look for tracks after a couple of days. Birds and squirrels usually come in through gaps or holes under tiles or timberwork at eaves level. Rodents like rats and especially mice can get in from just about anywhere, often gnawing small holes into holes large enough to enter easily.

Whilst these animals don't cause structural damage as such, they cause plenty of nuisance damage as they will gnaw timber, plastic pipes, and cables (sometimes killing themselves and your power in the process!). Plus, mess from droppings and nests will build up over time. Mice and rats will cause sanitary problems deeper in the house as they look for food. Birds and squirrels generally look for food outdoors.

Large nests are likely to be from squirrels, as they often like to stay in the same place for several generations.

It is important to wait until the nesting season is over and any young have left nests (or you risk trapping animals inside...). And even then, go into the nest area and make enough noise to scare away any animals present.

Fill in the entrance holes you identified plus any other holes you can find in your exterior walls to help prevent rodents getting in again. Old pipe holes, cable holes, broken vents, and gaps around doorframes. Don't forget any holes inside outbuildings such as garages or storage areas that join onto the main house.

Mortar or wire (chicken mesh) balled up and pushed or fastened into place works well and even wire wool or tin foil works in a pinch. Silicone sealants are also good for gaps, but are occasionally chewed, so keep an eye on those areas if you try it.

Clear away any old nests or debris.

TOP TIP Avoid leaving easy access to foodstuffs to deter exploring rodents (including maintaining strict rules when managing your waste/rubbish/garbage inside and outside your home).

TOP TIP Remove any old debris leaning up against the house (timber, pallets, garden stuff, tools etc.) as these provide 'runs' for rodents to move around unseen. Also cut back any branches or vegetation that overhang or are close to your roof to make climbing up there more difficult for squirrels particularly.

indoors

TOP TIP: Although it is largely a myth that an adult mouse can enter through a 6mm (1/4") hole, (although a 6mm (1/4") gap, maybe). Generally, though you'll need to block any holes from that size upwards to be safe.

TOP TIP: Remember that rodents will typically start looking for somewhere warm to nest as the temperature starts to cool in the autumn... Time any preventative maintenance well before this time of year.

BATS

CHECK: Watch your roof from outside at dusk in the summer time and you should see them leave or listen for the young bats 'chattering' at dawn when they are hungry and waiting for the adults to return and feed them.

Look out for droppings in your dark places (in the house, not your soul obviously!). Mouse droppings and bat droppings can look similar, but bat droppings crumble to dust when touched/crushed. Rodent droppings are more, erm... solid (eww!).

TO DO: Absolutely nothing! In fact, bats are useful creatures that don't cause any real damage to your home, no nests, no dangerous mess etc.

Enjoy sharing your home with these creatures or face a visit from your local constabulary, because they probably have more rights to be in your house than you do!

TOP TIP: However, if you have long term bat residents, it's a good idea to spread paper or cardboard underneath their roosting area (do this at night whilst they are out hunting) to protect your insulation and ceilings etc. from contamination by bat urine and droppings. Use the large packing rolls or those rolls of paper used on 'banqueting' tables etc. Anything absorbent will do the trick. Change the paper from time to time, wearing a tight-fitting breathing mask to avoid inhaling any dust.

EPILOGUE

How did you get on, what do you think?
Are you inspired to have a go at your maintenance?
I hope so!

You can really help other people (and me!) by leaving a review to let folks know what you think about the book, and how it could help them... Plus I'll be eternally grateful, and write more books!

author.to/ian (amazon.co.uk)
amazon.com/author/iananderson
goodreads.com/ian-anderson

It's taken me over 30 years working on the tools to gain enough experience to write this book, that's well over 50,000 hours. Phew. Still it'll only take you a few minutes to leave a review won't it. *wink*, *wink*...

GETTING IN TOUCH

For insults, typos you noticed, suggestions for revisions or general mudslinging, I'll look forward to hearing from you...

Please remember you're not alone. If you have questions, suggestions, or want to point out spelling mistakes or you just want to tell me about a better way. Please feel free to get in touch and I'll get back to you ......

CONTACT DETAILS

I'm happy to stand behind this book (and not only to avoid any eggs!) Of course, if this book makes heaps of money, I'll be far too busy on my boat to talk to you personally, but in that case, I promise I'll have one of my minions handle your enquiry...

For the foreseeable future however, I'd be delighted to hear from you. I'm always open to feedback and I'd love to read any constructive criticism you might have. I've taught myself everything I needed to learn to publish this book, so any errors you see are definitely my own.

If you're a spammer though, or overly rude, I'll have my men track you down...

You can email me at ian@handycrowd.com, or catch up with me on most flavours of social media...

facebook.com/handycrowd
twitter.com/handycrowd
pinterest.com/handycrowd
YouTube.com/c/handycrowd
linkedin.com/in/ianmanderson

COMPANION WEBSITE

You'll also find me pottering about on handycrowd.com where I'll be writing more 'how to' articles and answering your emails or comments.

Come on in, I'll go and put the kettle on!

SUBSCRIBE

You can also subscribe to receive updates whenever I post anything on the website and of course, I promise not to abuse your email address. I'll only write when there's something interesting or useful for you, Christmas's, and birthdays etc...

ABOUT THE AUTHOR

Hang on a sec. I'm not going to write this in the third person, because that's just silly, right? It's just me here after all, so here goes:

I'm an English builder and I've been self-employed since the tender age of 18. I was awarded a silver trowel at college for my skills with a trowel, as well as the silver medal, first prize for surveying and levelling, I'm now a Licentiate member of the City and Guilds Institute of London. Later I took a Master of Science degree in Trauma and Disaster Management from the University of Lincoln in the UK.

I've built new houses, extensions, restored period houses using lime mortars, underpinned ancient foundations, and restored centuries old roofing, as well as carrying out routine repairs and maintenance work on a variety of properties in the UK. I'm also a keen home mechanic and love classic cars. Oh, and I love recycling and repurposing stuff, especially pallets, my standard 'go-to' resource.

I'm a keen humanitarian and have lived and worked in various East African countries. In Uganda, I taught local artisans and built health units in remote rural areas, plus the restoration of a couple of hospitals. I also helped to set up projects in Rwanda as part of a British Conservative Party initiative by David Cameron for his international development team under Andrew Mitchell MP (project Umubano).

To balance things out I was a househusband or 'Mr Mom' for a couple of years; looking after 3 acres of wild New Zealand scrub, two chickens and of course my Norwegian wife, and two fantastic children.

I'm a 'try anything' handyman (or should that be 'repairperson' these days?) and it's my goal to learn something new every day. This I find very easy to do, as I'm writing, inventing, developing products and webmastering (all self-taught of course), close to the beach in Norway. And yes, of course, the days are never long enough...

Stay well, and I wish you well in all your own endeavours.

ANNUAL MAINTENANCE PLANNING NOTES

January	

February	

March

April

May	
June	

July

August

September

October

November

December

ADDITIONAL NOTES

ANOTHER BOOK BY IAN...

Imagine being able to do all your own stuff...

Fix broken things, improve your home, maintain stuff or even build new stuff from scratch.

...But you're afraid you don't have the skills.

Fear not, because this is a different kind of DIY book. It gently explains, it guides and motivates you far beyond 'do this, then do that'. You'll learn how to look at the physical world through 'practical eyes' like the professionals do. Copying real handy people, you'll learn as you go and get the job done.

There's over 30 years of professional experience as a builder and teacher in this actionable guide to being good with your hands and living a more practical life. It'll show you how to easily build your own skills and avoid all the common pitfalls.

So stop faking it with step-by-step instructions and be good with your hands for real.

You'll save money using your own head, hands, and heart to create something wonderful, fix something you treasure, maintain something you want to keep forever or build something just for fun.

You'll love being handy because then you can do anything!

Start being handy today, search for this title at an amazon near you.

Index

adjustments 6, 19
appliances 29, 97, 99, 100
Attic 100
Barge Boards 71
Basement 79
Bathroom 91
breakers 99
Cabinet 85
Ceilings 82
Chimney 76
cleaning 7, 8, 9, 10, 11, 18, 21, 23, 29, 31, 41, 42, 87, 96
Doors 84
Drains 59
drywall 82
Extract Fans 94
fabric 46, 50, 90
Fascia 71
Faucets 94
flooring 80
friction 7, 11, 19, 21, 24, 26, 46, 49
fuses 99
gutters 36, 37, 51, 64, 70, 71
heating 80, 91, 92, 97, 103
Indoors 79
Insulation 101
Kitchen 85
kitchen sink 59, 61, 86, 95
Leaks 100
Loft 100
lubricants 7, 8, 11, 12, 13, 16, 17, 83
maintenance-free 3
Masonry 26, 31, 63, 65
metals 25, 26, 27, 40, 44, 45
Mould 93

Outdoor 58
Overflows 98
Pipes 37, 96, 98
plaster 36, 41, 82
plastic 5, 24, 26, 32, 37, 38, 45, 46, 48, 60, 62, 63, 69, 73, 87, 88, 92, 95, 96, 105
refrigerator 87
roof 5, 30, 32, 36, 37, 39, 59, 72, 73, 74, 75, 76, 80, 94, 98, 100, 101, 103, 104, 106, 107
rubber 17, 24, 38, 39, 46, 47, 48, 49, 59, 60, 61, 62, 63, 69, 70, 71, 75, 90, 93, 94, 95, 96
rust 6, 14, 25, 26, 27, 40, 43, 44, 45, 55, 78
schedule 10, 23, 51, 52
service 5, 6, 17, 22, 23, 24, 97
Silicone 91
switch 95, 99, 100
Taps 94
timber 2, 29, 30, 31, 59, 60, 68, 69, 72, 83, 92, 102, 104, 105, 106
Tumble Dryer 90
Unwanted Creatures 104
Valleys 75
Vegetation 67
vehicle 5, 13, 15, 41, 46, 53, 54, 55
Ventilation 103
Verges 71
Walls 81
Washing Machine 89
Water Traps 95
Windows 82

Printed in Great Britain
by Amazon

58726745R00078

Liz Ashworth is is Scottish food heritage. She has written a number of books, including the Teach the Bairns to Cook series, as well as newspaper and magazine features. She also writes the monthly blog for Gordon Castle Walled Garden. Liz has been involved in developing award-winning products, particularly in the field of healthy eating. She helps create special food events for the Orkney International Science Festival and can be seen cooking in her own kitchen on Youtube.

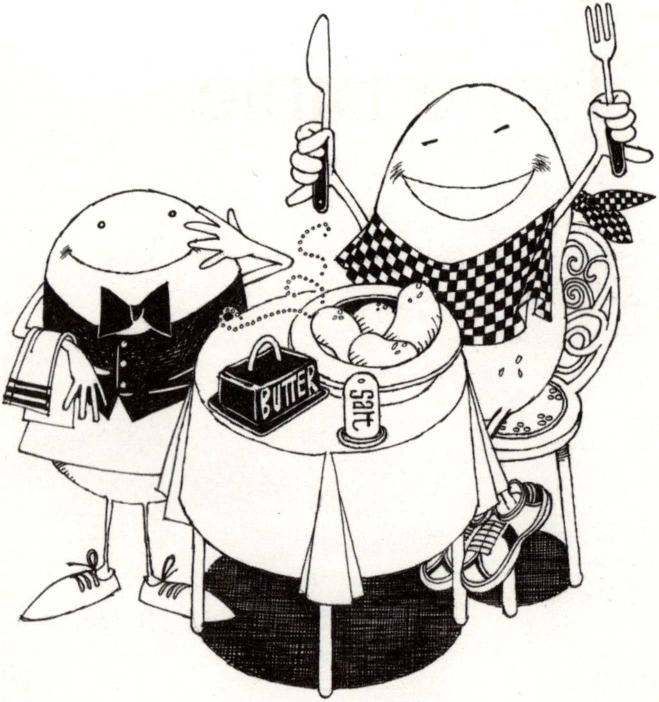
BUTTER
Salt

The *Scottish* Tattie Bible

Liz Ashworth

Illustrated by Bob Dewar

BIRLINN

This edition first published in 2024 by
Birlinn Limited
West Newington House
10 Newington Road
Edinburgh
EH9 1QS

www.birlinn.co.uk

Copyright © Liz Ashworth 2017
Artwork copyright © Bob Dewar 2017

First published in 2017 as *The Willliam Shearer Tattie Bible*

The moral right of Liz Ashworth to be identified as the
author of this work has been asserted by her in accordance
with the Copyright, Designs and Patents Act 1988

All rights reserved. No part of this publication may be
reproduced, stored or transmitted in any form without
the express written permission of the publisher.

ISBN: 978 1 78027 899 5

British Library Cataloguing-in-Publication Data
A catalogue record for this book is available
from the British Library

Designed and typeset by Mark Blackadder

MIX
Paper | Supporting
responsible forestry
FSC® C018072

Printed and bound by Clays Ltd, Elcograf, S.p.A.

Contents

Introduction	11
About tatties	16

How to cook a tattie
Boil	22
Steam	23
Mash (Champit tatties)	24
Bake	25
Roast	27
The ultimate chip	29
Sauté potato (Fried tatties)	31
Potato gratin	32
Home-made tattie crisps	34

Traditional tattie recipes
From Scotland
Clapshot	36
Clapshot pies	36
Burns Supper starter	37

Rumbledethumps	38
Colcannon	39
Kailkenny	40
Champ	40
Sam's hairy tatties	41
Hairy tatties with garlic and olive oil	43
Stovies	44
Orkney pattie	46
Mince 'n' tatties wi' a tattie doughball	48
Doughballs	49

From further afield

Spudnuts – two ways	50
Bombay potatoes	52
Boxty in the pan	53
Scandinavian potato casserole	55
Patatas bravas	56
Mutti's bohnengemüse	58

Brunch

Tattie scones	60
Grate tattie oat pancakes	61
Hash bean browns	63
Bacon floddies	64
Granny Mac's fish cakes	65
Sausage, bacon and apple rolls	67
Tattie omelette	69
Tattie salad	71
Swabian kartoffelsalat	72

Soups
Cullen skink	74
Potato, celeriac and apple soup	75
Vichyssoise	76
Spicy tomato and tattie soup	78
Twenty-minute tattie and leek soup	79
Wee dumplings	80

Main meals
Scots potato pies	82
Posh fish pie	84
Harry's one-pot pheasant	86
Dounby saus 'n' cheesy tatties	87
Cotter's Saturday night pie	89

Puddings
Tattie lemon tart	93
Little lemon puds	94
Raspberry tattie bakewell	95

Baking and confectionery
Potato oatcakes for cheese	98
Tattie and spelt crispbreads	100
Potato, apple and cinnamon loaf cake	101
Fruity tattie buns	102
Lefse (Norwegian potato pancakes)	103
Canadian potato candy	105
Misread macaroon bar	106
Chocolate tattie truffles	107

Gluten-free
Chocolate potato fudge brownies 109
Chocolate potato fudge topping 110
Mashed tattie gluten-free dropped scones 111

Mabel Thomson's tattie wine 112

'What I say is that, if a man really likes potatoes, he must be a pretty decent sort of fellow.'

A.A. Milne

'The potato is the most valuable gift the new world ever gave to the old.'

Dr Cramond, Cullen in
The Elgin Courant, 1899

Introduction

'Lord look o'er us, three tatties among four of us.
Thank God, there's nae mair o'us.'
From *We'll Say the Blessing*, Catriona Monro

In 1954 our family moved to a new house on the outskirts of Elgin. Creating a garden was hard work. At a weekly rate of three 'pennies', my sister and I helped remove endless stones and grass roots. Dung arrived. Dusty Miller the gardener came and planted 'tatties to clean the soil'.

We waited. Patience brought her reward – how good were those tatties! That first pot of freshly boiled Duke of York tatties, their floury interior bursting, nutty flavoured, through golden skin, began a lifelong affinity. I love all tatties, some more than others: Sharpe's Express, Keppleston Kidneys, Pink Fir Apple, Golden Wonders, even the new Bikini!

And the Westray Tattie! On a trip to the island, I was dared to eat a steaming bowlful and duly obliged. At the ferry the following day, the farmer arrived to deposit a large bag of said tatties in the boot. Oh those tatties!

In 1868 Orcadian store-owner Thomas Warren sold Westray tatties for two shillings a barrel. He was my great-great-grandfather.

The potato was brought to Europe from Peru by the Spanish during the sixteenth century. There was in some countries, including Scotland, initial prejudice against the crop. Eventually around 1690 potatoes began to be grown in a few Scottish gardens but not in the open field until 1739, when 'persons travelled long distances to examine the new crop' (*The Elgin Courant*, 1899).

There was much to commend the potato. It helped eliminate chronic debilitating scurvy. Safely grown underground, less labour-intensive and providing a higher yield per acre, the potato provided a welcome alternative to grain crops, which often failed due to poor weather.

In 1783 the Icelandic volcano Laki erupted and a cloud of poisonous gas spread over Europe. Barley and oats withered in the field. At Lochlie Farm in Ayrshire, Robert Burns and his family had a hard time: 'The summer of 1783 was brutal' (*A Biography of Robert Burns* by James Mackay).

Kirk sessions, as guardians of the poor, were interested in the culture of potato. In 1783, with famine persisting, the session of Grange bought and distributed ten guineas' worth of turnip and potato seed, considering the importance of such crops in 'present scarcity'. Reluctance to grow the crop gradually dispelled and the tattie became an important dietary staple, often referred to as 'meat'.

In 1845 potato disease hit Ireland and the Icelandic volcano Hekla became active. When the disease affected Orkney some thought volcanic ash the cause. A writer describes 'dust so thick on the heather as to dim the bloom'. However, 'potatoes have never had such fine flavour, even in a good season since the disease began.'

The potato's ability to grow in poor soil and weather in the Highlands and Islands caused almost total dependence on it for food. This led to famine in 1846, when blight destroyed the crop and did so for several years. Many chose emigration to Canada or Australia, some assisted by the 'Laird'. A stark contrast to the violent evictions of the Clearances.

Agricultural practice improved and, with research, the emergence of disease-resistant varieties. In 1882 Colorado beetle devastated the American crop and Scottish seed potatoes were imported, up to 40,000 tons annually, mainly from Dundee. The boom lasted for 30 years from 1882 till 1912.

The Victorians embraced the potato, serving elaborate dishes. Shooting lunches often called for two hundred-weight of baked potatoes carried to the moors packed in sacks and skewered together to trap heat.

Potato rationing was not necessary during the Second World War due to a good home-grown supply, and the 'Potato Pete' campaign encouraged people to eat more because of their nutritional value.

The role of children in harvesting was important, hence the school October 'tattie' holidays. Children worked in the fields with their families lifting (howking) the tatties following a device aptly named a 'digger'. Many enduring friendships were made between families working in the tattie fields.

Today, mechanisation has taken the effort out of the potato harvest. The back-breaking labour of 'tattie howking' is a distant memory, and the 'tattie holidays' are simply a break from school. However, so good are our tatties that quality Scottish seed potatoes are grown all over the UK and also exported.

Home-grown tatties have sustained generations and the Scottish housewife must be congratulated on her creative skills.

It is amazing what you can make, bake or brew with a humble tattie.

This book is filled with information, tips and recipes to enhance your tattie experience. There is guidance on how to cook tatties from plain boiled to the ultimate chip. There are classics like rumbledethumps, stovies and the Orkney pattie. Recipes from further afield include patatas bravas and bohnengemüse, a family recipe never before recorded – and new ones, specially created for this book. A buried treasure indeed!

The recipes are graded according to their tattie rating (ease of making) and type of potato.

Tattie rating

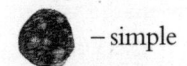

– simple

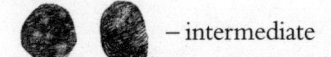

– intermediate

– more difficult

Type of potato

W – Waxy
F – floury
AR – all-rounder
N – new

About tatties

'*Money* is the root of all evil, and yet it is such a useful root that we cannot get on without it any more than we can without potatoes.'

– Louisa May Alcott,
novelist (1832–88)

Tattie
The Scots call the potato a 'tattie'. Spelling and pronunciation vary – tatty, tatteh, tatie, taati, tatae, tatte, tautie, tawtie, tatoe, tattoo, tatta, tottie are a few.

Potatoes are good for you
An excellent source of plant protein, vitamins C and B6, they are free of fat, sodium and cholesterol. At around 110 calories per 100 grams (31 calories per ounce), potatoes are only fattening when cooked in fat/oil or eaten in large quantities. Naturally gluten-free, they contain iron, manganese, magnesium, phosphorus, copper, and more potassium than a banana. They are a good source of carbohydrate and fibre.

The healthiest way to eat potato is with the skin left on,

limiting nutrient loss in cooking, be it boiled, steamed or baked.

Tattie types
- Dry mealy potatoes with a high starch content cook to a dry, floury, fluffy texture.
- All round multipurpose potatoes with a medium starch content are used for most cooking methods.
- Waxy, moist potatoes containing less starch and more sugar are 'stickier' and firm when cooked.

Which type of tattie? Drop it in brine made of one part salt to eleven parts water. Waxy potatoes float, dry potatoes sink.

Heritage
Renewed interest in heritage varieties has seen the return of potatoes first grown over a century ago – for example:

Duke of York (1891) – mealy texture, full flavour and golden flesh.
Sharpe's Express (1901) – recognised by its pear shape and white fluffy flesh.
Pink Fir Apple (1850) – pink-skinned tubers of yellow waxy flesh.
Kerr's Pinks (1917) – floury, soft with excellent flavour. Originally grown in 1907 by J. Henry, Cornhill, Banff.
Golden Wonder (1904) – pale cream floury flesh. Boils rapidly, makes great chips!

Shetland Black – said to have come from a 1588 Spanish Armada shipwreck. Dark purple skins, intensely dry flesh and native to Shetland.

Red Emmalie, Highland Burgundy, and others too many to mention, all distinctive in appearance, flavour and cookability.

For more information, see *www.thompson-morgan.com/potato-selector-guide*, or William Shearer's Seed Potato Catalogue at *www.williamshearer.co.uk*.

Scottish seed potatoes are exported all over the world.

Grow your own

Growing potatoes in planters or grow bags is the perfect solution if you want to grow your own but have limited space. There's nothing like freshly dug home-grown tatties – even for Christmas!

See *www.thompson-morgan.com/how-to-grow-potatoes-in-bags* for step-by-step instructions.

Buying

Buy locally, in season.

Storing

Treat with care; potatoes bruise easily. Remove from polythene bags to avoid sweating. Keep in a cool, well aired, dark place. Exposure to light produces green skin containing a toxin: do not eat.

Cooking tips

- Add peeled raw potato to over-salted mince, soups or stews to absorb excess salt. Remove before serving.
- Thicken soups, stews and casseroles with mash.
- Save cooking water for soups and gravies.
- Drop peeled potatoes into lightly salted water to retain colour.

Bakers' tips

Pastry – potato pastry handles well, bakes evenly and retains crispness.

Victoria sponge – a spoon of mash beaten in with the eggs prevents curdling.

Rich cakes – add a spoon of mash while creaming fat and sugar. The cake will bake more evenly, cut without crumbing and stay moist longer.

Oatcakes – added mash makes an easy roll-and-cut dough, which bakes evenly crisp.

Gluten-free

Potato flour – a creamy flour ground from the whole potato. It readily absorbs liquid. Use sparingly in breads, cakes and scones.

Potato starch – this is an allergen-free white powder which does not stand up to prolonged heat so is best used to thicken sauces toward the end of cooking. Use a balloon whisk. Added to baked goods it gives lightness. Use sparingly.

Other uses in the home

- Rub scalds with a slice of raw potato.
- Clean potato peel soothes swollen eyes.
- Potato water helps clean silver.
- Raw potato and bicarbonate of soda can remove stains and rust.
- Dry potato peel thrown on a fire saves coal.
- Potato juice makes good invisible ink.

Why are potatoes called spuds?

A false origin is that it came from the nineteenth-century group called Society for the Prevention of an Unwholesome Diet – SPUD – who were against eating several foods including potatoes.

It may come from an old English name for the sharp narrow digging spade which is called a spud. Or possibly from the Dutch *spyd*, Norse *spjot* or Latin *spad*, meaning sword or dagger. The exact derivation is unknown.

How to cook a tattie

Benny

Boil

'The Scottish housewife at least knows how to boil a potato. Curiously, a perfectly boiled potato is a thing that is rarely to be had in the most expensive hotels and restaurants. They simply will not steam them dry.'

– F. Marian McNeill, *The Scots Kitchen*

Tips
Potato skin prevents the flesh being waterlogged in boiling, thereby retaining nutritional value, flavour and texture.

Cooked unpeeled potatoes keep longer in the fridge.

Peel potatoes thinly: most food value is directly under the skin.

Boil slowly to cook potatoes through evenly.

Potatoes of similar size will be cooked at the same time.

If boiled potatoes discolour, add a little lemon juice or vinegar to the cooking water.

Steam foil-wrapped fish or chicken and vegetables over potatoes for economy.

New potatoes
Scrub or scrape the delicate skin.

Cook in gently boiling salted water for 15–20 minutes till tender. Drain, steam and serve at once with butter and freshly chopped parsley.

Oatmealie tatties
Toss freshly boiled potatoes in butter, shake in a handful of toasted oatmeal, scatter with fresh parsley. A family favourite.

Crushed new tatties
Roughly crush with butter or olive oil, add herbs or spices. Serve hot.

Maincrop potatoes
Cover with cold water, add sea salt and boil, then reduce the heat to simmer to cook evenly. Potatoes are cooked when the point of a knife or skewer slides through. Drain through a colander or sieve, and shake. If possible take the pan and lid to open (cold) air, lift lid up and down a few times to create steam and dry the potatoes without losing heat. Cover with a dry tea towel or kitchen paper to absorb steam.

Benny's tattie tip
Neighbour Aubrey puts his pan of drained tatties on the doorstep to fluff – a tip learned on the family farm in County Armagh from his father Benny. It works. Cold air opens starch cells on the surface.

Steam
Thinly peeled or still in their jackets, old and new potatoes.

Steam over simmering salted water, 15 to 20 minutes for new potatoes and up to 30 minutes for maincrop, depending on size and variety.

Mash (Champit tatties)

Sheer indulgence – the ultimate comfort food.

Use floury or all-round maincrop like Maris Piper or King Edward. Boil potatoes of similar size, unpeeled or peeled thinly. Cover in cold salted water. Boil and simmer slowly till the point of a skewer goes smoothly through the flesh. Drain through a colander or sieve, shake, steam covered with a clean towel. Peel if needed. Mash or pass through a potato ricer or sieve.

For 450g (1lb) potatoes beat in 2 tablespoons of warm milk and 30g (1oz) of soft butter till smooth and fluffy. (Over-beating produces a gluey texture.) Taste, season and serve.

Mash can be stiff or soft depending on the potatoes and preferred taste. Potato puree is made by blitzing with added cream and/or melted butter to a sauce-like consistency.

Jazz up mash
Try the following: smoked cheese and chive; garlic and black pepper; grated lemon rind and olive oil; cooked mashed celeriac or parsnip.

Be adventurous, keep note of successes.

My top favourites are avocado or smooth stewed apple.

Dietary challenged mash
Beat with dairy-free milk or some of the cooking water. Add olive oil for a creamy finish.

Bake

A baked potato has a fluffy interior and a crisp skin. Serve with or without a filling of which there are many.

The basics
Allow 1x 225g (8oz) potato per person (F/AR).
Scrub clean. Prick skin. Rub with oil and salt.

Baking options
Oven bake
Heat the oven to 200°C (fan 180°C), 400°F, Gas 6. Bake on the oven shelf or a tray for 1½ hours.
For speedier spuds parboil for 15 minutes, then drain, prick the skin, oil, salt, and bake for 40 to 45 minutes.
Half the potato lengthwise, lay flat on an oiled tray, bake for 25 to 35 minutes.
Microwave the prepared potato for 5 minutes, then oven bake for 45 minutes.

Slow cooker
On high power for 4½ hours, on low for 7½ hours.

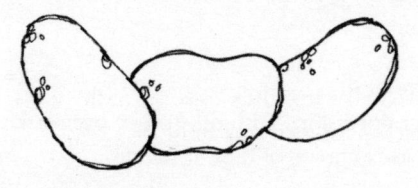

Microwave

Run under the cold tap, wrap each potato in kitchen paper, then cook on high for 3 or 4 minutes, turn and repeat. If a fork goes in easily, but the core is still a little firm, the potato is ready. Best to undercook, as an overcooked potato may burn or explode! Rest for 5 minutes for the heat to cook the centre and fluff the inside.

Barbecue

Foil wrap. Bake for 1 to 2 hours. Parboil to cut time.

To serve, up end, cut a cross on top, push in the sides and ends gently to fluff open, ready for butter!

A few ideas

Simply fill

Split and add cheese, coleslaw, baked beans, tuna mayo, grated cheese with chopped bacon.

Loaded potato skins

Split, scoop out, leaving 5mm (¼in.) rim. Mash flesh with cheese and bacon. Pile in skins, oven bake or grill crisp. Serve hot, topped with sour cream and chopped chives.

Crispy potato skins

Brush scooped skins with oil, grill or oven bake to crisp. Serve with a choice of dips or fillings.

Roast

Varieties like Maris Piper, King Edward, Golden Wonder, potatoes with a high starch content, make crisp roasters. Check new varieties on: *www.thompson-morgan.com/potato-selector-guide*.

Serves 4
600g (1lb 5oz) potatoes, thinly peeled and cut to even size (F/AR/N)
Sea salt
2 tablespoons oil or fat

Suitable roasting temperature from 180°C (fan 160°C), 350°F, Gas 4 to 200°C (fan 180°C) 400°F, Gas 6, allows an organised cook to fill the oven.

Cover the potatoes with cold salted water, boil for 8 to 10 minutes. Drain through a colander or sieve, and shake well to fluff. If liked, score with the prongs of a fork, creating important cracks which roast crisp.

Suitable fats and oils

Oils – rapeseed, sunflower, grapeseed, corn, olive, flavoured oils.

Fats – duck, goose, lard, dripping, or suet and salt.

Heat the 2/3 tbsp oil/fat in a heavy baking tray or roasting tin. Shake the potatoes into the hot oil/fat and turn to coat. Roast till golden, turning occasionally. Drain on kitchen paper in a heated dish and serve. Keep crisp in a warm oven for 15 minutes.

Skinny roasters

Brush parboiled potatoes with oil. Roast on a non-stick tray, turning occasionally.

New potatoes

No need to parboil. Roast small even-sized potatoes in their jackets. Turn frequently.

The ultimate chip

I worked weekends in the Larder at Rothiemurchus while my son Alan and his friend James helped at the fish farm nearby. On our homeward journey we began our quest for the ultimate chip. Armed with a list of venues, we ticked off another each week. From soggy, half-cold to golden crisp we tried them all – some more than once!

A good chip is a joy to eat. It should have a fluffy centre with outside crunch, crisp to the last chip.

The basics
Use floury or medium floury potatoes – Maris Piper, King Edward, Golden Wonder. Waxy potatoes make soggy chips. Thick chips are less fattening than thin or crinkle. Parcooked chips can be kept for up to one day in the fridge.

Serves 2 to 3
600g (1lb 5oz) potatoes, washed
2 litres (3½pt) groundnut, sunflower or corn oil
Sea salt

Peel on or peeled, cut thick or thin chips.
Rinse in cold water, drain, and dry on a clean tea towel.

Frying method

Use a large pan and chip basket or free-standing fryer. Only fill the pan one third – oil rises as it cooks. Be safe. Have a fire blanket or extinguisher near.

Heat the oil in the fryer to 130°C or till a raw chip begins to float and fry. Cook small batches.

Half-fill the chip basket, lower into the oil and fry slowly till the chips are tender but not browned. Drain on kitchen paper. Heat the oil to 180°C or till a chip turns golden and crisp. Lower in the chips to fry till crisp and golden. Drain on kitchen paper, serve at once sprinkled with sea salt.

Parboil method

Cover the chips in cold salted water, boil, then simmer for 5 minutes. Drain, shake dry and cool on a wire rack. Heat the oil to 140°C. Fry the chips till just colouring. Drain on kitchen paper. Heat the oil to 180°C, fry till golden. I found chips made by this method stay crisp longer.

Oven chips

Cut thick chips, soak for 10 minutes in cold water, drain and dry. Heat the oven to 200°C (fan 180°C) 400°F, Gas 6. Oil a heavy baking tray, heat for 3 minutes. Put the chips in one layer on the tray and brush with oil. Bake for 20 minutes, turning once or twice. Drain on kitchen paper and serve.

Sauté potato (Fried tatties)

Sauté means to cook quickly, from the French *sauter*, to jump.

Allow 225g (8oz) sliced potatoes per person, cooked or raw (F/AR/N)
Butter or oil
Choose a thick-bottomed frying pan

Sauté raw potato
Cut peeled or unpeeled potatoes into 5mm (¼in.) slices, soak in cold water, drain and dry on kitchen paper. Fry at medium heat for 5 minutes on each side till golden and cooked through. Some potatoes take longer than others. Drain on kitchen paper and serve.

Sauté cooked potato
Cut cooked potato, with or without peel, into 5mm (¼in.) slices. Fry for 2 or 3 minutes on each side till crisp. Some potatoes colour faster than others. Drain on kitchen paper and serve.

New potatoes
Cut raw or cooked small new potatoes in half lengthwise before frying.

Potato gratin

If ever there was a kitchen game, set, and match, it is a potato gratin.

Gratin is defined as 'baked with encrusted browned surface'. The traditional heat-resistant dish is shallow and sloping sides mean a wider surface for the all-important crust.

Sliced, grated or shredded, potato absorbs flavour as it bakes.

A basic recipe for a simple gratin from the Canadian *Potatoes* booklet of 1958.

Serves 4

1 medium onion, peeled and thinly sliced
30g (1oz) butter
4 medium potatoes, peeled and thinly sliced, shredded or grated (F/AR/W/N)
Sea salt
Ground black pepper
120ml (4fl oz) water or stock
85g (3oz) grated cheese
30g (1oz) breadcrumbs
15g (½oz) butter if liked

Turn on the oven at 180°C (fan 160°C), 350°F, Gas 4. Sweat the onion in butter till soft. Butter a suitable dish. Starting and ending with potatoes, layer with the onions, seasoning each. Pour stock or water over the dish and bake covered for 25 to 30 minutes. Mix the cheese and breadcrumbs. Remove the dish cover, sprinkle with the cheese and crumbs. Turn the temperature to 200°C (fan 180°C), 400°F, Gas 4. Bake the gratin for 10 minutes to brown or crisp under a medium hot grill.

Try adding
Chopped ham or bacon
Smoked haddock and tomato
Sliced mushrooms
Chopped chicken or turkey
Replace water with stock, double cream, or a pouring white or cheese sauce

Get gratin-ing!!

Home-made tattie crisps

Once made in Orkney in several flavours, Pomona Crisps had a certain home-made quality about them. Bring them back!

Serves 4

2 medium-size potatoes, peeled and thinly sliced (F/AR) – use a mandolin if you have one
Oil or dripping to deep fry
Sea salt

Put the potato slices in a bowl under slow running cold water for 30 minutes. Drain and dry thoroughly on kitchen paper. Heat the oil to 180°C, 350°F or till a slice of bread takes 1 minute to brown slowly in the oil. Prepare a tray covered in kitchen paper. Deep fry in small batches. Turn frequently with a slotted heat-resistant spoon. It will take 2 or 3 minutes for the slices to become golden. Drain on kitchen paper. Enjoy freshly fried, sprinkled with sea salt. Store on kitchen paper in a sealed container.

Microwave

Lay potato slices on a suitable oiled plate. Brush with oil. Microwave on high power in 30 second bursts. Turn as needed. Remarkable results – try it.

From one tattie many crisps grow.

Traditional tattie recipes

From Scotland

Clapshot

Traditionally served at Burns Suppers and Harvest Homes.

Serves 4
Takes 15 minutes to make

450g (1lb) potato, cooked in boiling salted water,
    drained and steamed dry (F/AR)
450g (1lb) turnip, cooked in boiling salted water and drained
60g (2oz) butter
Finely chopped chives or spring onion
Sea salt and ground black pepper

Melt the butter in a deep saucepan, add the potatoes and turnip. Mash together, then beat smooth with a wooden spoon. Season to taste with plenty of ground black pepper and sea salt. (Some add a pinch of ground ginger.) Stir in the chives. Serve hot. If the turnip is pale, add a little carrot or sweet potato while cooking.

Clapshot pies
Cover mince, stew or haggis with clapshot. Sprinkle with grated cheddar and oven bake at 180°C (fan 160°C), 350°F, Gas 4 for 25 minutes.

Burns Supper starter

Spoon haggis into buttered ramekin dishes, top with clapshot. Oven bake for 10 minutes. Serve hot.

Rumbledethumps

'Rumble' means mashed together and 'thump' to bash down. This traditional Borders dish is like Scottish bubble and squeak!

Serves 2
Takes 25 minutes to make

225g (8oz) cold cooked mashed potatoes (F/AR)
185g (6oz) cold cooked cabbage or sprouts – some recipes add turnip
30g (1oz) butter
1 small onion or a few spring onions, peeled and chopped
Sea salt and ground black pepper
60g (2oz) grated mature cheddar cheese

Melt the butter in a deep pan, add the onion and cook on low heat to soften. Add the potatoes and cabbage or sprouts, 'rumble and thump' together, season to taste. Turn into a buttered ovenproof dish, top with the grated cheese and brown under a pre-heated grill. Serve hot.

Add extra 'rumble'
Stir in: cooked meat, chicken, turkey, cooked bacon, smoked fish, or baked beans.

Colcannon

Traditional mash from the Highlands.

Serves 4
450g (1lb) mashed potatoes (F/AR)
450g (1lb) cold cooked carrot, turnip and cabbage, mashed together
60g (2oz) butter
2 teaspoon brown sauce
Sea salt and ground black pepper

Melt the butter in a pan, add the potatoes and vegetables. Keep stirring over medium heat to mix till bubbling. Season to taste with salt, pepper and brown sauce. Serve hot.

Kailkenny

The name is thought to be a corruption of Colcannon.

Serves 2
225g (8oz) cold mashed potato (F/AR)
225g (8oz) cold cooked cabbage
3 tablespoons double cream
Sea salt and ground black pepper

Mix the potatoes and cabbage together, beat in the cream and heat slowly, stirring continuously, over medium heat. Season to taste and serve very hot.

Champ

Beat creamy mashed potatoes (F/AR) with plenty butter and chopped spring onions and serve hot.

Sam's hairy tatties

Similar continental dishes are described as emulsions of salt fish, oil and potatoes. 'Hairy Tatties' says it all!

An Orkney take on the classic by chef Sam Britten.

Serves 4 as a starter

Step 1
150g (3½oz) salt fish soaked in cold water for 24 hours

Step 2
300ml (½pt) milk
½ shallot, peeled
1 bay leaf
500g (1lb 2oz) potatoes, peeled and cut into small pieces (F)
200g (7oz) butter
185g (6oz) white crab meat

To serve:
Home-pickled cucumber or small gherkins
Shallots, peeled and cut in thin rings
Fresh lemon juice
Parsley oil – see overleaf

Simmer the drained salt fish in milk with the shallot and bay leaf for 15 to 20 minutes. Remove the fish and flake. Strain and reserve the milk. Boil the potatoes in salted water till very tender. Drain, steam dry, then pass through a ricer or sieve. Beat the warm potatoes with butter (allow 50g (1¾oz) butter to 100g (3½oz) potato) to emulsify. Heat the finished mash by stirring over low heat, adding a drop of reserved milk to prevent it from splitting. Treat the finished mash like mayonnaise because of the high fat content. Beat in the flaked salt fish and crab meat (as much or as little as you like). Beat off the stove until you see fish fibres making it 'hairy'.

Serve a small amount in the centre of a bowl with home-pickled cucumbers, parsley oil and fresh shallot rings dressed in lemon juice.

Parsley oil

Blanch a handful of fresh parsley in boiling salted water for 10 seconds. Drain, then drop in iced water. Drain, blitz with olive oil to a smooth green puree. Store sealed in the fridge.

Hairy tatties with garlic and olive oil

Thank you to Catherine Brown for this recipe taken from her book *Scottish Seafood: Its History and Cooking*.

Serves 4

Step 1
500g (1lb 2oz) heavily salted fish, soaked 12 to 24 hours depending on saltiness

Step 2
300ml (10fl oz) extra virgin olive oil, warmed
4–6 cloves garlic
500g (1lb 2oz) potatoes, cooked and mashed (F)
50ml (4 tablespoons) hot milk
1 tablespoon chopped fresh parsley

Drain the fish, cover with cold water, boil, turn off the heat, cover and leave for 15 to 20 minutes. Cool, lift onto a plate, and remove bones. Put into a food processor, add garlic and a little warm oil, blend for a few seconds and repeat with the rest of the oil. Add the parsley and whiz till smooth. Pour into a bowl, beat in the mash and whisk in the hot milk till light and 'hairy'. Taste and season. Serve with warm toast and poached or boiled eggs.

Stovies

F. Marian McNeill (*The Scots Kitchen*, 1929) suggested 'to stove' has French origins. However Catherine Brown (*Scottish Cookery*, 1985) discovered there is a Scottish and North of England word 'stove'. It means a slow sweated, steamed stew cooked in a covered pot.

No matter, the recipe is not precise, more a satisfying versatile one-pot meal.

The basics

Serves 4
1.1kg (2½lb) potatoes, peeled and thickly sliced (F/AR)
2 medium onions, peeled and sliced
45g (1½oz) fat – bacon, dripping, butter or oil
Water or stock
Sea salt and ground black pepper
Pinch of nutmeg or allspice

Choose a strong deep pan with tight-fitting lid. Heat the fat, add the onion and potato. Stir together, cover and cook on low heat for up to 10 minutes. Stir frequently. Add a little water, stock or gravy. More liquid makes wetter stovies. Stir, cover, cook on low, stirring occasionally, till the potatoes start to disintegrate.

Add chopped cooked meat or fish. Season to taste with salt and plenty black pepper. Add nutmeg or allspice if liked.

Different tastes

Make browned pieces of potato to mix through by cooking to a crisp layer on the pan base then stir through.

Add a little liquid, and steam uncovered for dry stovies. Beat well, adding more gravy or sauce to taste to make a smooth, softer eat.

Stovies tried and tested

Roast beef – dripping, add roast gravy and chopped beef to taste.

Roast turkey – created and cooked over a campfire for cubs who queued for seconds begging to scrape the pan! Add chopped roast turkey or chicken and gravy. Leftover stuffing too, if liked.

Cullen skink – butter, onion, chopped smoked haddock, double cream and black pepper. Winner of the 'Exotic Stovie' prize, Huntly Hairst 2012.

Corned beef – beat in chopped corned beef, and brown sauce or gravy.

Try – black pudding, haggis, sausages, mince, stew, chickpeas, smoked salmon.

What will you add to the stovie pot?

Orkney pattie

What is an Orkney pattie? Every Orkney chipper has its secret family formula but, despite extensive 'in the chippie' research, its origins remain elusive.

Makes 10 patties
85g (3oz) leftover mince mixed with
1 small onion, peeled, chopped and lightly fried
450g (1lb) mashed potato (F/AR)
60g (2oz) fresh breadcrumbs
Sea salt and ground black pepper
Oil to deep fry

Batter
60g (2oz) self-raising flour
¼ teaspoon salt
Scant 200ml (7fl oz) cold water

Mix the mince, onion, potato and breadcrumbs together, season with salt and plenty of black pepper. Shape into patties (a thick round scone-shape), 60g (2oz) weight. Dust with flour and chill for at least 30 minutes. Sift the flour and salt into a bowl, whisk in the cold water to make a smooth batter, rest for 30 minutes. Heat the oil to 180°C or till a slice of bread turns golden in 1 minute. Flour the patties if sticky, dip into batter to coat and slide into hot oil. Fry for 5 minutes, turning to brown evenly. Drain on kitchen paper and serve hot with chips. Patties can be frozen before battering and cooked from frozen at 170°C for 6 to 8 minutes to ensure they are cooked through.

A joy of indulgence only fully appreciated eaten fresh from an Orkney chipper!

Mince 'n' tatties wi' a tattie doughball

Interviewed on Radio Scotland's *Kitchen Café*, accordionist Phil Cunningham admitted that a plate of 'mince 'n' tatties' is his taste of home.

Serves 4
450g (1lb) steak mince
1 medium onion, peeled and chopped
45g (1½oz) oatmeal
Sea salt
Ground black pepper
Boiling water

Cook the mince in a saucepan on medium heat, stirring with a wooden spoon to brown and separate the meat grains. Add the onion and stir to brown a little. Lower the heat, stir in the oatmeal with enough water to make a rich gravy. Simmer covered for 35 minutes. Stir occasionally to prevent sticking, adding water if needed, taste and season. Make doughballs.

Doughballs

Makes 4
85g (3oz) self-raising flour
1 level teaspoon baking powder
¼ teaspoon sea salt
30g (1oz) mashed potato (F/AR)
45g (1½oz) suet
Water

Sift the flour, baking powder and salt into a bowl. Add the mashed potato and suet and fork together. Mix to a soft elastic dough with cold water. Turn onto a floured board, divide in four and shape each into a soft ball. Stir the mince, adding more water if needed to ensure plenty gravy. Gently drop into the simmering mince, cover to trap steam, which will cook the dumplings. Leave for 12 to 15 minutes till firm and soaked in gravy.

Serve with mash – see page 24.

From further afield

Spudnuts – two ways

Across the pond a song was written about delivering 'spuds':

> *It's Bud the spud from the bright red mud*
> *Rollin' down the highway smilin'*
> *The spuds are big on the back of his rig*
> *And they're from Prince Edward Island.*

Named after Spudnut, once a chain of doughnut eateries.

Makes 7 doughnuts
115g (4oz) self-raising flour
1 teaspoon baking powder
60g (2oz) butter or margarine
60g (2oz) mashed potato (F/AR)
1 small teaspoon vanilla essence or 1 level teaspoon mixed spice or ground cinnamon
30g (1oz) caster sugar
1 small egg, beaten
Caster sugar to coat

To oven bake

Turn on the oven at 190°C (fan 170°C), 375°F, Gas 5. Oil a heavy baking tray. Sift the flour and baking powder into a bowl. Add the butter and mashed potato and fork together. Stir in the sugar. Mix to a soft light dough with the beaten egg. Heat the baking tray for a few minutes. Turn the dough onto a well-floured board, sprinkle with flour and flatten with the palm of your hand to 1cm (½in.) thickness. Cut with a round 6cm (2½in.) cutter. Rework scraps lightly. Lay on the hot tray. Bake for 10 to 12 minutes till risen and golden. Shake the caster sugar on a sheet of baking paper. Toss the hot spudnuts in sugar one at a time, pressing the sugar in gently. Cool on a wire tray. Enjoy warm and freshly baked.

To deep fry

Heat oil to 180°C, 350°F or when bread takes a minute to brown in the oil. Cook doughnuts for 3 minutes on each side till cooked through. Toss in caster sugar, cool on a wire tray and serve warm.

Spudnuts stay soft for 24 hours and can be frozen in a sealed container for 4 weeks.

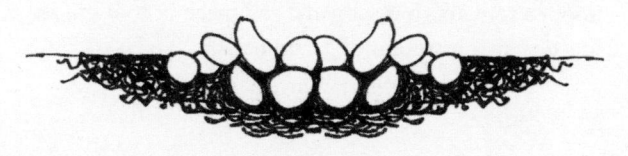

Bombay potatoes

Over 30 years ago I joined a group of like-minded housewives to make, bake and sell. We called ourselves Polmont Crafts. One, Anne, grew up in India; this is her recipe.

Serves 4
375g (12oz) cooked potatoes cut into quarters (F/AR/W/N)
2 tablespoons cooking oil
½ teaspoon mustard seeds
½ teaspoon cumin seeds
¼ teaspoon turmeric
¼ teaspoon chilli flakes
¼ teaspoon sea salt
1 tablespoon hot water
Chopped fresh coriander to serve

Heat the oil in a pan on medium heat. Drop in a few mustard seeds – when they pop add the seeds and spices. Stir for 1 minute then add salt and potatoes. Stir fry for 4 minutes. Turn the heat to low, add water and cover the pan. Steam for 5 minutes. Serve hot scattered with chopped fresh coriander.

May be eaten in a sauce made with 115g (4oz) chopped tomato, clove of garlic and piece of root ginger blitzed with 1 teaspoon of garam masala.

Boxty in the pan

Boxty is a traditional Irish potato pancake. Its popularity inspired the rhyme:

Boxty on the girdle, and boxty in the pan,
The wee one in the middle is for Mary Anne.
Boxty on the girdle, and boxty in the pan,
If you can't bake boxty sure you'll never get a man.

Makes 8 pancakes
100g (3½oz) grated raw potato (F/AR)
100g (3½oz) mashed potato (F/AR)
115g (4oz) plain flour
½ teaspoon sea salt
10g (2 teaspoons) baking powder
2 eggs, beaten
75ml (2½fl oz) milk to mix
Oil or butter to fry

Put the grated potato into a clean cloth, twist and squeeze to remove moisture. Sift the flour, salt and baking powder into a bowl. Add the grated and mashed potato, eggs and enough milk to make a stiff batter. Heat a heavy frying pan on low to medium heat. Add a tablespoon of oil or butter. Do not overheat the pan. These thick pancakes must be cooked for 3 to 4 minutes on each side to avoid raw middles! A timer is handy. Drop tablespoons of batter into the pan and flatten a little with the back of the spoon. Cook for 3 minutes or till bubbles rise and burst on the surface. Turn to bake for 3 or 4 more minutes till cooked through. Drain on kitchen paper. Serve hot. Traditionally eaten spread with butter and a sprinkling of sugar, and at breakfast fried as part of the famous Ulster fry.

Modern recipes add spices, herbs and garlic.

Scandinavian potato casserole

A warm smooth light soufflé, which does not collapse!
Real comfort food that leaves you wishing there was more.

Makes a starter for 4 or light meal for 2
300g (10oz) cooked, riced or mashed potatoes (F/AR)
60ml (4 tablespoons) milk
Single cream to mix
¼ teaspoon sea salt
Ground black pepper
Pinch of nutmeg (optional)
30g (1oz) grated parmesan or similar hard cheese
2 eggs, separated

Turn on the oven at 180°C (fan 160°C), 350°F, Gas 4. Butter 4 x 10cm (4in.) ramekins. Beat the potatoes smooth with the milk and one tablespoon of cream. Beat in the seasoning, egg yolks and cheese to a smooth dropping consistency, adding more cream if needed. Beat the egg whites stiff and fold in. Pour into the ramekins. Bake in a water bath for 15 to 20 minutes till risen and golden. Serve hot as a starter. Alternatively, pour into a buttered 75ml (1¼pt) soufflé dish and bake for 25 to 30 minutes till risen and golden. Enjoy hot.

Patatas bravas

In 1933 Madrid, a small bar called Las Bravas served fried potatoes with spicy tomato sauce, creating 'patatas bravas'. The dish has gone international!

Serves 4 people
750g (1lb 10oz) potatoes, peeled and cut into bite-size pieces (F/AR/N)
Sea salt
15ml (1tbs) olive oil

Turn on the oven at 200°C (fan 180°C), 400°F, Gas 4. Cook the potatoes in boiling salted water for 5 minutes. Drain through a sieve or colander, shake dry. Heat a heavy baking tray in the oven. Toss the dry potatoes with olive oil and scatter in a single layer on the hot baking tray. Roast for 15 to 20 minutes till brown and crisp, turning once. Meanwhile make the sauce.

Tomato (brava) sauce
15ml (1 tablespoon) olive oil
1 medium onion, peeled and chopped
2 cloves garlic, peeled and crushed (optional)
½ teaspoon smoked paprika
Pinch of cayenne pepper
½ teaspoon balsamic or sherry vinegar
1 tin chopped tomatoes (225g/8oz)
Sea salt

Heat the olive oil in a pan on medium heat, sweat the onion and garlic till soft. Stir to prevent sticking. Add paprika, cayenne, vinegar and tomatoes. Simmer for 15 minutes. Taste and season. Serve chunky or blitz smooth.

Quick sauce
Stir paprika, cayenne, crushed garlic and sherry vinegar into tomato ketchup to taste.

Drain the potatoes on kitchen paper, toss into a heated bowl and sprinkle with sea salt. Serve sauce on the side. Provide eaters with small plates, a spoon and fork.

Mutti's bohnengemüse

I leave my friend Gisela to tell the story:
> My grandmother was born in Alsace-Lorraine. My grandfather was an engineer in the coalmines; he and his young family came to the Ruhr district around 1910. This recipe came with them and is only known and loved in my family. I don't know more about it. German bohnenkraut is important for flavour.

Mutti (Gisela's mother) made the best. I love it.

Serves 4

450g (1lb) floury potatoes, peeled and sliced thinly (F)
450g (1lb) onions, peeled and sliced
450g (1lb) tomatoes, skinned and sliced
450g (1lb) whole fresh young green beans, topped and tailed
450g (lb) lean pork, trimmed and cut into slices
Sea salt
Ground black pepper
Handful of summer savory (bohnenkraut), thyme or oregano
150ml (¼pt) vegetable stock or water

Use a deep heavy pan or casserole. Layer the vegetables on top of the pork, adding herbs, seasoning as you go. Pour in the stock or water. Cover tightly. Cook slowly for at least 2 hours on very low heat on the cooker. Check occasionally, add more liquid if needed but do not stir. Alternatively, oven cook at 140°C (fan 120°C), 275°F, Gas 1.

Slow cooking is important. Serve hot in warm bowls with crusty bread and a glass of pils.

Brunch

Tattie scones

Each June, at Piping Hot Forres, the World Tattie Scone Competition (inspired by the late David Urquhart) invites lovers of this delicacy to be creative.

My neighbour, Rev. Bill Miller, was partial to a tattie scone, warm from my kitchen – a simple recipe with potential!

Makes 8 scones

225g (8oz) plain boiled potatoes mashed smooth or pressed through a ricer (F/AR)
Approximately 60g (2oz) self-raising flour
15g (½oz) melted butter
¼ teaspoon sea salt
Milk if needed to mix

Heat a heavy frying pan or girdle on medium. Put the potatoes, butter, flour and salt into a bowl. Stir together, adding milk if needed to make a light smooth dough. Turn onto a floured board and knead gently. Half, and work into two balls. Roll each to a thin circle on a floured board. Cut both into four triangles. Test the girdle heat with a sprinkle of flour. If it's too hot it will burn; golden brown shows the pan is ready. Bake the scones for 3 minutes on each side. Keep warm in a clean tea towel on a wire tray. Enjoy warm. Equally good fried as part of a traditional breakfast.

Riced potatoes make lighter scones.

Grate tattie oat pancakes

My cooking friend Moira and I concoct recipes to demonstrate in the food fayre at the annual Nairn Show. This one was a hit.

Serves 4
225g (8oz) cooked potato, roughly grated (F/AR/W)
1 small carrot, peeled and finely grated
1 tablespoon porridge oats
1 teaspoon grated lemon rind
1 egg
Sea salt
Ground black pepper
Butter or oil to cook

To serve:
4 fresh eggs at room temperature
4 slices black pudding
Freshly chopped parsley

In a bowl mix the grated potato and carrot and the oats, season with sea salt and ground black pepper and grated lemon rind. Mix with the beaten egg. Boil a pan of salted water and reduce the heat to below simmer. Heat a tablespoon of butter or oil in a large frying pan on medium heat. Drop 4 tablespoons of potato mixture into the pan, pressing with the back of the spoon to make a flat pancake. Cook for 3 minutes on each side. Drain on kitchen paper. Keep warm while frying the black pudding till crisp on each side. To poach the eggs, break each into a teacup and slide into the hot water for 3 to 4 minutes. Do not boil. Serve each pancake on a warm plate, topped with black pudding and a softly poached egg. Garnish with chopped parsley.

Nairn Show

Hash bean browns

At our annual Guide camp we took turns to cook. A memorable concoction involved frying tatties and baked beans over the fire. This version omits smoke flavour and twigs!

Serves 4
500g (1lb 2oz) chunks of cooked potato, roughly crushed (F/AR)
45g (1½oz) butter, smoked bacon fat or oil
½ onion, peeled and finely chopped
Sea salt and ground black pepper
1 small tin of baked beans, drained

Heat a heavy frying pan at medium. Melt half the fat, stir in the onion to soften, add the potatoes, season and stir together. Add the drained beans and stir in. Press together to make a pancake, and cook for 10 minutes or till the underside forms a thick browned crust. Take a flat plate large enough to cover the pan, loosen the potato pancake, then invert the pan to deposit the pancake on the plate, browned side up. Melt the rest of the fat, and slip the pancake back in the pan for another 8 to 10 minutes to brown. Cut into quarters and serve hot.

Store in the fridge for up to 3 days.

Bacon floddies

As a result of famine in the mid 1800s, total dependency on potato as a food crop waned. The excess fed pigs instead – perhaps inspiration for this rhyme:

Holy Brethren, is it not a sin? To put tattie peelings into the bin. The peel feeds pigs – The pigs feed you – Now Holy Brethren, is that not true?

Serves 2

225g (8oz) potato, peeled and grated (F/AR/N)
1 small onion or a few spring onions, peeled and chopped
85g (3oz) smoked bacon, chopped
30g (1oz) self-raising flour
1 large egg, beaten
Sea salt and ground black pepper
Oil or bacon fat to fry
Grated cheese

Put the grated potato into a clean tea towel, twist to squeeze out excess liquid. Shake the potato into a bowl, season, mix in the chopped onion, bacon and flour. Stir in the egg. Heat the oil or fat in a frying pan at medium heat. Drop tablespoons of mix into the pan to cook for 3 or 4 minutes on each side till golden. Slow fry to ensure each floddie is cooked through. Drain on kitchen paper. Serve hot topped with grated cheese.

Granny Mac's fish cakes

Mrs Kate Maclaren (Granny Mac) was pre-war Principal of the Girls' Technical School in Elgin. Her son Donald and my father were close friends, and when Donald emigrated to Canada, Granny Mac became part of our family. A signed copy of her cookery book published in 1938 has been handed down. This is her recipe.

Makes 4 x 85g (3oz) fish cakes
225g (8oz) mashed potato (F/AR)
115g (4oz) flaked flesh of an Arbroath Smokie
10g (¼oz) melted butter – add more to drier mash
Sea salt and ground black pepper
Plain flour
Beaten egg to coat
Breadcrumbs to coat
Butter or oil to cook

Put the mash into a bowl, fork together with the flaked fish and melted butter, taste and season. Divide into five equal portions. Shape into round flat cakes on a floured board. Chill for 10 minutes. Make a production line. Pour beaten egg on a plate, next breadcrumbs on a sheet of baking paper, lastly a clean plate. Dip each fish cake into egg, drain, lay in the crumbs, use paper to lift and coat, press the crumbs lightly into the surface, lift onto the plate. Shallow fry in melted butter, oil or a mixture, at medium heat for 4 minutes on each side till golden. Drain on kitchen paper and serve with lemon mayonnaise.

Lemon mayonnaise
Sister Sue's recipe, Granny Mac would approve!

Beat grated lemon rind and juice into mayonnaise to taste. Season and serve.

Sausage, bacon and apple rolls

A spur-of-the-moment recipe.

Makes 18 cocktail-size rolls

Pastry:
115g (4oz) self-raising flour
45g (1½oz) mashed potato (F/AR)
60g (2oz) margarine
Pinch of sea salt

Filling:
100g (3½oz) pork sausage meat
75g (2½oz) smoked bacon, finely chopped
30g (1oz) tangy eating apple, finely grated
Ground black pepper
Beaten egg, to glaze

Turn on the oven at 180°C (fan 160°C), 350°F, Gas 4. Use a food processor or mixer to blend pastry ingredients into a clean dough. Alternatively, rub the margarine into the flour, stir in the potato and knead together. Leave to rest. Mix the filling ingredients together. Shape into two sausage-like lengths on a floured board. Lay on a plate. Cut pastry in half. Roll each piece to a rectangle approximately 30cm x 15cm (12in. x 6in.). Brush with beaten egg. Lay the sausage 1cm (½in.) from the long edge of each. Lift the pastry over the sausage and roll into a cylinder across the strip to seal, ending with the join underneath. Divide each roll into 9 and lay on a baking tray. Cut a slit on top of each, brush with beaten egg. Bake for 15 to 20 minutes till crisp. Enjoy hot or cold.

Mix a teaspoon of chutney or pesto in the filling instead of apple.

Tattie omelette

My late father was a dab hand at whisking up a mean omelette. Spanish tortilla and Italian frittata are, in my humble opinion, not a patch on Dad's.

Serves 2

225g (8oz) cooked potato, cut into bite-sized pieces (F/AR/W/N)
15g (½oz) butter
4 large eggs, beaten with 2 tablespoons milk
Dash of Worcestershire sauce – Dad's taste secret
Sea salt and ground black pepper
115g (4oz) cheese slices

Heat the butter in a 24cm (9½in.) frying pan at medium heat. Add potato and keep stirring to brown lightly. Spread evenly over the pan. Turn on the grill at medium. Beat the eggs, milk, sauce, salt and pepper together. Pour the egg mixture into the pan. Using the flat blade of a palette knife, gently draw egg inwards from the pan edge so that the egg runs through the potato and cooks. While the top is still runny, quickly lift under the grill for a few seconds to set. Top with overlapping slices of cheese. Grill to melt, bubble and brown. Serve from the pan with a simple tomato salad.

Soufflé style

Separate the yolks and whites of two eggs. Beat egg yolks and milk together. Whisk whites stiffly and fold into the egg mix. Cook as above. The cheese puffs as it melts – yummy.

Tattie salad

Pouring dressing over warm tatties adds depth of flavour to a salad.

Serves 4
550g (1lb 4oz) potatoes (AR/W/N)
1 tablespoon white wine or cider vinegar
½ teaspoon sea salt
Ground black pepper
1 tablespoon chopped fresh chives or spring onions
1½ teaspoon each of mayonnaise and Greek yoghurt mixed together

Boil the potatoes in salted water till tender, drain well. Mix the vinegar, sea salt, ground black pepper and half the chives and pour over the warm potatoes in a bowl and shake gently. Infuse for 1 hour. Gently mix in the rest of the chives and mayonnaise mix. Serve garnished with a few snipped chives.

Tarragon, chervil or parsley may also be added. Store sealed in the fridge for up to 2 days.

Swabian kartoffelsalat

My friend Gisela writes: 'According to my family in Stuttgart this potato salad is the most savoury in Germany.'

Serves 6
750g (1lb10oz) scrubbed small new potatoes

Dressing:
Pinch of sugar
¼ teaspoon sea salt
A little white pepper
2 tablespoons onion, finely chopped
2½ tablespoons cider vinegar
60ml (2fl oz) vegetable stock

To finish:
5 tablespoons olive oil

Cook the potatoes in boiling salted water till tender. Drain. Slice into a bowl when cool enough to handle. Mix the dressing ingredients and pour over warm potatoes, shake to coat, infuse for 20 minutes, stir in oil and serve. *Guten appetit!*

Soups

Cullen skink

I learned to make Cullen skink in the kitchens of Baxter's staff canteen. The secret lies in a 'floury tattie' which disintegrates to a satisfying gloopiness as the soup pot simmers. Original recipes use Finnan haddock, involving removal of fish bones. Smoked fillet makes life easier for the soup maker.

Serves 4

1 onion, finely chopped
550g (1lb 4oz) potatoes, peeled and chopped (F)
450ml (¾pt) creamy milk
600ml (1pt) water
450g (1lb) undyed smoked haddock fillet
30g (1oz) butter
Sea salt and ground black pepper
150ml (¼pt) double cream (optional)
Chopped fresh parsley or chives to garnish (optional)

Put the onions and potatoes into a deep soup pot, pour in the milk and water, bring to the boil, reduce the heat, cover and simmer for 40 to 45 minutes or till the potatoes are softly disintegrating. Lay the fish on top of the soup, cover to simmer for 5 minutes till the fish is cooked. Reduce the heat, flake the fish through the soup, stir in the butter and season to taste. Serve hot, garnished with freshly chopped parsley or chives and a swirl of cream.

If not sufficiently thick, stir in some mash.

Potato, celeriac and apple soup

During the 1970s I shared a flat at Innes House, near Elgin, and made friends with other residents over shared meals, wine and chat. We remain in touch. Delicious soup served at our last party inspired my friend Veronica to experiment. The result is stunning.

Serves 4
15ml (1 tablespoon) vegetable oil
225g (8oz) potato, peeled and chopped (F/AR)
350g (12oz) celeriac, peeled and chopped
115g (4oz) eating apple, peeled, cored and chopped
1 stick celery, cleaned and chopped
30g (1oz) root ginger, peeled and chopped
1 litre (1¾pt) vegetable or chicken stock
Lemon juice
Sea salt and ground black pepper
Nutmeg

To serve:
Chopped toasted walnuts
Crumbled stilton cheese

Heat the oil in a deep pan on medium heat, add the vegetables, apple and ginger, and stir to soften. Add the stock, boil, reduce the heat to simmer covered for 45 minutes till tender. Blitz smooth, season to taste, adding a pinch of nutmeg and squeeze of lemon juice to enhance flavour. Serve hot topped with walnuts and/or stilton!

Vichyssoise

Friends invited two couples for dinner on consecutive weekends, but confusion with dates caused 'double booking'. Hostess Joy had made vichyssoise sufficient for the extra diners but was short of one portion for herself. A professional actress, used to improvising, she passed off a plate of cold milk topped with chopped grass as one of the best soups she had ever made. The diners wholeheartedly agreed, and even asked for the recipe!

Serves 4
15g (½oz) butter
60g (2oz) onion, chopped
60g (2oz) white leek, shredded
60g (2oz) celery, finely chopped
1 litre (1¼pt) vegetable stock
450g (1lb) potatoes, peeled and cubed (F/AR)
Sea salt and ground black pepper
120ml (4fl oz) double cream
Chopped chives

Melt the butter in a deep pan on low heat. Add the onion, leek and celery. Stir for 2 minutes to soften but not colour. Add the potato, stir to soften for 2 minutes. Add the stock, boil and reduce the heat to simmer for 30 minutes. Blitz smooth and season to taste.

Traditionally served cold
Softly whip the cream and fold into the chilled soup. Serve garnished with chopped chives.

Served hot
Stir in double cream and adjust seasoning. Serve hot garnished with chopped chives and/or parsley.

Spicy tomato and tattie soup

The Portsoy Co-op raises funds for charity at a soup and sweet lunch in the hall. The Station Hotel across the road is always pleased to provide soup. Feedback for this one was positive.

Serves 4

2 tablespoons olive oil
1 large onion, peeled and chopped
185g (6oz) carrot, peeled and chopped
85g (3oz) turnip, chopped
450g (1lb) potato, peeled and chopped (F/AR)
2 fresh garlic cloves, peeled and crushed
5cm (2in.) root ginger, peeled and chopped
2 x 250ml (8fl oz) cartons of sieved tomato
600ml (1pt) vegetable stock
Sea salt
Ground black pepper
1 teaspoon smoked paprika

To serve:

Chopped parsley
Double cream

Heat the oil in a deep pan on medium, add the vegetables, potatoes, garlic and ginger and stir to soften for 3 minutes. Add the tomato and stock. Boil, reduce to simmer covered for 45 minutes. Blitz smooth, season with sea salt, ground black pepper and smoked paprika.

Serve hot with a swirl of double cream (if liked) and chopped parsley.

Twenty-minute tattie and leek soup

Invented coming in late from a frosty shopping trip. My lunch guest Jim and I emptied the pan – the sign of a good soup!

Serves 2
85g (3oz) leeks, finely chopped
45g (1½oz) onion, chopped
85g (3oz) carrot, finely grated
175g (6oz) potato, grated (F/AR/W)
2.5cm (1in.) root ginger, peeled and chopped
750ml (1¼pt) stock or water
Sea salt and ground black pepper

Put the vegetables and ginger into a deep pan, add the water or stock and boil. Cover, lower the heat to simmer for 20 minutes. Ladle a third of the soup into a bowl and blitz smooth. Return to the pan, season to taste and re-heat. Serve hot with oatcakes.

Wee dumplings

An optional extra, found in an old book.

Makes 8 hazelnut-size dumplings
50g (1¾oz) mashed potato (F/AR/W)
30g (1oz) oatmeal
1 level teaspoon baking powder
Sea salt and ground black pepper
Broth from soup

Mix the mash, oatmeal and baking powder, and season. Mix to a stiff dough with broth. Roll into hazelnut-size balls. Drop into simmering soup, cover, steam for 5 minutes. Serve in the soup.

Main meals

Scots potato pies

A 'no pastry' pie, peculiar to Scotland, with many regional variations.

Serves 2
2 large potatoes of equal size, peeled thinly (F/AR)
1 tablespoon dripping or oil

Filling:
115g (4oz) minced cooked meat – beef, lamb, venison, chicken or game
1 small onion, peeled, chopped, blanched for 5 minutes in boiling water and drained
Brown sauce or gravy
Sea salt
Ground black pepper

Turn on the oven at 200°C (fan 180°C), 400°F, Gas 6. Put the dripping/oil in a deep-sided baking tin into which the potatoes fit with room to crisp. Cut a 5cm (1in.) top off each potato. Hollow the centre, leaving a rim of 1cm (½in.). For stability cut a small slice from the base of each. Mix the meat and onion, moisten with brown sauce/gravy, season to taste. Fill each potato and replace the tops. Heat the baking tin for 2 minutes. Stand the potatoes upright in the tin and baste with fat. Roast for 1 hour, basting occasionally. Test with the point of a skewer after 45 minutes; some potatoes cook more quickly. Serve hot with gravy.

Other fillings
Minced chicken and ham
Cumberland sausage
Haggis

Banffshire potato pies
For this variation, make a filling with 60g breadcrumbs, 1 egg yolk, chopped herbs, a little milk and melted butter. Grated cheese or flaked smoked haddock may be added.

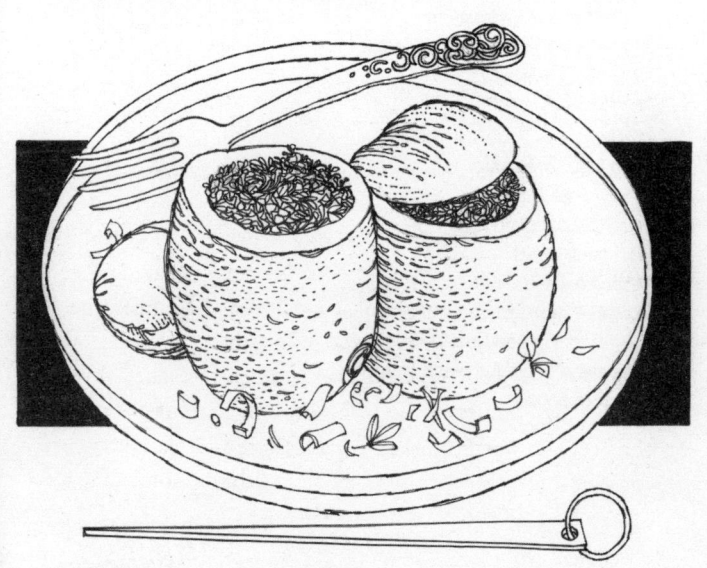

Posh fish pie

This pie travels well. Its prototype survived a drive to Aberdeenshire where lunch guests gave it twelve marks out of ten!

Serves 4 to 6
85g (3oz) fresh salmon fillet
85g (3oz) fresh hake or other firm white fish
Bay leaf
A few peppercorns
Generous squeeze of fresh lemon juice
450ml (15fl oz) milk
115g (4oz) fresh haddock
115g (4oz) smoked haddock fillet
85g (3oz) prawns

Sauce:
30g (1oz) margarine
15g (½oz) butter
45g (1½oz) plain flour
Poaching liquid
Milk if needed
15ml (1 tablespoon) fresh lemon juice
10g (¼oz) grated hard cheese
Sea salt and ground black pepper
Pinch of nutmeg

Topping:
450g (1lb) potatoes, peeled and cut into cubes (F/AR)
15g (½oz) melted butter
225g (8oz) celeriac, peeled and cut into cubes
10g (¼oz) grated hard cheese

Turn on the oven at 180°C (fan 160°C), 350°F, Gas 4. Butter a wide pie dish 20cm x 25cm (8in. x 10in.). Put the salmon and hake, bay leaf, peppercorns, lemon juice and milk into a pan. Boil, lower the heat to simmer for 4 minutes. Add the haddock, simmer for a further 4 minutes. Turn off the heat. Meanwhile cover the potatoes in cold salted water, boil, lower the heat to simmer till tender. Cook the celeriac in boiling salted water till tender. Lift the fish onto a plate, discard the bay leaf and peppercorns. Reserve the milk. Cut the fish into chunky pieces, check for bones and set aside. Make a sauce by melting the margarine and butter together on low, add flour and stir to a smooth paste. Use a balloon whisk to beat in the fishy milk to make a pouring sauce. Add more milk if needed. Stir in the cheese and lemon juice, season with salt, pepper and nutmeg. Fold in the fish and pour into the prepared dish. Drain the potatoes, steam dry, mash with melted butter. Drain the celeriac well, mash smooth. Beat into the potato then spread over the fish. Dust with cheese. Bake for 30 minutes till crisp on top. Serve with salad and plum tomatoes.

Harry's one-pot pheasant

My neighbour Harry likes pheasant; his wife Iris less so. An oversupply of the bird gave me food, or should I say 'game' for thought! They both enjoyed the result.

Serves 2

300g (10oz) pheasant – leg and thigh, skinned, trimmed
15g (1 tablespoon) cornflour, seasoned with sea salt and ground black pepper
60g (2oz) onion, finely chopped
1 eating apple, peeled, cored and chopped
1 small stick celery, finely chopped
350g (12oz) potatoes, peeled and sliced (F/AR/W/N)
Sea salt
Ground black pepper
300ml (½pt) vegetable or chicken stock

Turn on the oven at 150°C (fan 130°C), 300°F, Gas 2. Toss the pheasant in seasoned cornflour. Put half the pheasant into the base of a casserole dish, add half the apple and celery, cover with a thin layer of potato. Season and repeat. Finish with a thicker layer of sliced potato. Pour the stock over. Season lightly. Cover, cook slowly for 1 hour 45 minutes. Turn oven to 180°C (fan 160°C), 350°F, Gas 4. Remove lid to brown the top for 15 minutes. Serve scattered with chopped parsley.

Dounby saus 'n' cheesy tatties

Dounby Primary teacher Nicola Moar created this recipe with her cooking class, using the Dounby butcher's sausages, Orkney butter, milk and cheese, Westray Fairtrade chutney and Birsay tatties grown by school bus driver Ronnie Ballantyne.

Didn't they do well!

Serves 4
8 butcher's sausages, cooked and sliced
600g (1lb 5oz) boiled potatoes, cooled and sliced (F/AR/W/N)
2 dessertspoons chutney

Sauce:
45g (1½oz) butter
45g (1½oz) plain flour
500ml (16fl oz) milk
115g (4oz) mature Orkney cheddar cheese
Sea salt and ground black pepper

Topping:
45g (1½oz) oatmeal
30g (1oz) fresh bread crumbs
115g (4oz) crumbled farmhouse cheese

Turn on the oven at 160°C (fan 140°C), 325°F, Gas 3. Butter a medium-size lasagne dish. Melt the butter, stir in the flour to a smooth paste, and gradually stir in the milk.

Keep stirring till the sauce boils and thickens. Lower the heat, stir in the cheese, season to taste and remove from the cooker. Layer half the sliced potatoes in the base of the dish, pour a quarter of the sauce over and cover with the sliced sausages. Spread with chutney and cover with the rest of the potatoes. Pour over the remaining cheese sauce. Mix the oatmeal and breadcrumbs and sprinkle over along with the crumbled cheese. Bake for 20 to 25 minutes till bubbling and the top is crisp. Serve hot.

Cotter's Saturday night pie

Burns's 'The Cotter's Saturday Night' made me wonder what the frugal wife had in her larder. Neeps, carrots, leeks, tatties, oatmeal in the girnel, milk and butter 'frae the coo!'

But now the supper crowns their simple board …
The dame brings forth, in complimental mood,
To grace the lad, her weel-hain'd kebbuck, fell;
And aft he's prest, and aft he ca's it guid:

Serves 4

Base:
150g (5oz) mince
45g (1½oz) onion, finely chopped
115g (4oz) carrots, peeled and diced
60g (2oz) turnips, peeled and diced
45g (1½oz) leeks, finely chopped
30g (1oz) oatmeal
Water
Sea salt and ground black pepper

Topping:
225g (8oz) grated cooked potato (F/AR/W/N)
45g (1½oz) oatmeal
45g (1½oz) crumbly farmhouse cheese
15g (½oz) butter

Turn on the oven at 180°C (fan 160°C), 350°F, Gas 4. Butter a pie dish 20cm x 25cm (8in. x 10in.). Put the mince in a saucepan, stirring with a wooden spoon to brown and separate the meat grains. Add the onion, stir to brown a little. Mix in the vegetables and oatmeal. Stir in sufficient water to cover, boil, lower the heat, cover and simmer for 45 minutes, stirring occasionally. Add water if needed. Season to taste and pour into the pie dish. Mix the grated potato, cheese and oatmeal and scatter on top and dot with butter. Bake for 25 minutes till browned and bubbling. Serve hot with oatcakes.

May ye 'aft ca' it guid'!

Puddings

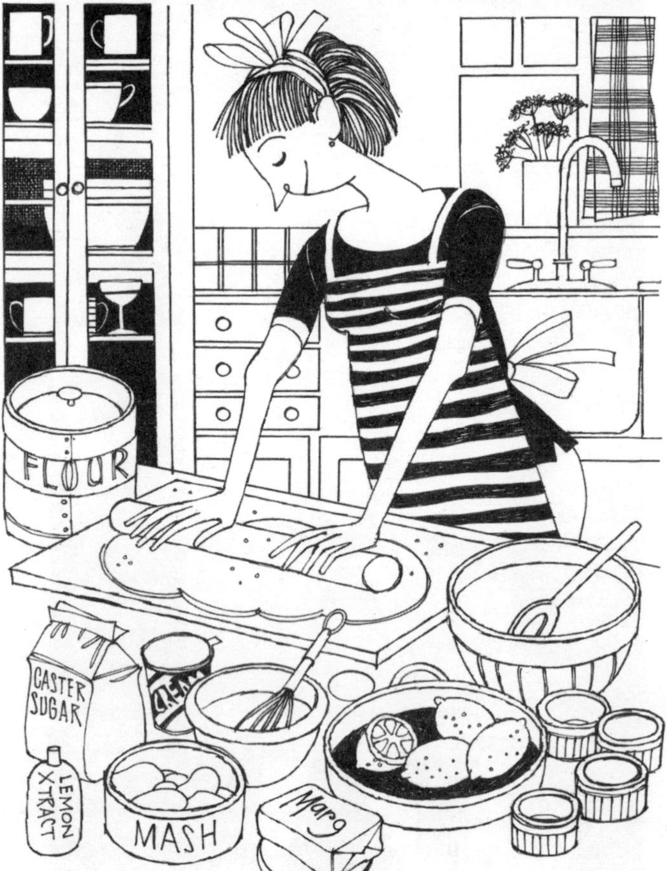
FLOUR
CASTER SUGAR
LEMON XTRACT
MASH
Marg

Tattie lemon tart

A classic, tangy pudding compared with sweeter lemon meringue pie.

Makes a 20cm (8in.) round tart

Pastry:
115g (4oz) self-raising flour
45g (1½oz) mashed potato (F/AR)
60g (2oz) margarine
15g (½oz) caster sugar

Filling:
2 large eggs
85g (3oz) caster sugar
Zest of 1 lemon
Juice of 1½ lemons
1 teaspoon lemon extract
100ml (3½fl oz) cream
60g (2oz) warm boiled potato, riced or mashed (AR/W)

Turn on the oven at 190°C (fan 170°C), 375°F, Gas 5. Put the pastry ingredients in a mixing bowl and fork into a dough. Turn onto a floured board, knead smooth and roll out to line a 20cm (8in.) diameter tart tin. Prick with a fork, chill for 10 minutes. Bake blind for 12 to 15 minutes, remove the lining and bake for 5 to 10 minutes to dry. Remove from the oven and lower the heat to 150°C (fan 130°C), 300°F, Gas 2. Beat the eggs, sugar, lemon rind, lemon juice and extract together in a bowl. In a separate bowl beat the cream and potato till smooth. Beat the lemon and potato mixes together. Pour into the tart case. Bake for 30 minutes till set. Serve warm or chilled.

If liked, strain lemon mix to remove rind before adding to the potato mix.

Little lemon puds
Pour the filling into buttered ramekins. Bake in a water bath for 20 minutes till set. Serve warm or chilled.

Raspberry tattie bakewell

From a recipe restricted by wartime rationing.

Makes a 20cm (8in.) round tart

Pastry:

115g (4oz) self-raising flour
45g (1½oz) mashed or riced potato (F/AR)
60g (2oz) margarine
15g (½oz) caster sugar

Bakewell filling:

60g (2oz) margarine
60g (2oz) caster sugar
60g (2oz) cooked mashed potato
1 egg
1 teaspoon vanilla or almond essence
60g (2oz) self-raising flour sifted with 1 level teaspoon baking powder
1 tablespoon raspberry jam

Turn on the oven to heat at 180°C (fan 160°C), 350°F, Gas 4. Put the pastry ingredients into a bowl, fork into a dough. Turn onto a floured board, knead smooth and roll out to line a 20cm (8in.) round tin. Cream the margarine and sugar till light, beat in the potato, egg and essence, then fold in the sifted flour and baking powder. Spread the jam on the pastry base. Cover evenly with sponge mixture. Bake for 20 to 25 minutes till firm and golden or the point of a skewer inserted in the middle comes out clean. Dust with caster sugar. Serve warm with cream or custard as a dessert or serve cool, drizzled with lemon water ice, as a tea cake.

Lemon water ice
Mix sifted icing sugar with fresh lemon juice to a thin smooth paste. Drizzle off a spoon or the prongs of a fork.

Baking and confectionery

Potato oatcakes for cheese

For those who find oatcake making a challenge, add potato. A dream to knead, roll and cut, baking to an even crisp. Delicious warm from the oven with or without cheese!

Makes 60 x 5cm round biscuits
225g (8oz) fine or medium oatmeal
60g (2oz) mashed or riced potato (F/AR)
3g (½ teaspoon) sea salt
1g (scant ¼ teaspoon) bicarbonate of soda
26ml (scant 2 tablespoons) vegetable oil
Water to mix
Oatmeal or rice flour to roll out

Turn on the oven at 180°C (fan 160°C), 350°F, Gas 4. Use a food mixer. Put the oatmeal, potato, salt, bicarbonate of soda and oil into the mixing bowl. Mix on slow speed, gradually adding tepid water in stages, until a smooth pliable clean dough is formed. The sound of the mixer will change as the dough comes together. Turn out the dough and dust with oatmeal or rice flour. Knead smooth. Roll out thinly and cut into 5cm (2in.) round biscuits. Put onto a non-stick baking tray. Alternatively divide the dough into four pieces, roll each into a thin round and cut across the diameter to make 4,

6 or 8 triangles depending on desired size. (Scots refer to the triangles as farls and the round of dough a bannock.) Bake for 12 to 15 minutes till crisp and cool on a wire rack. Store sealed in an airtight container.

Add flavour
1 teaspoon rough black pepper
5g (1 teaspoon) grated hard cheese
1 teaspoon dried mixed herbs or 1 tablespoon of fresh

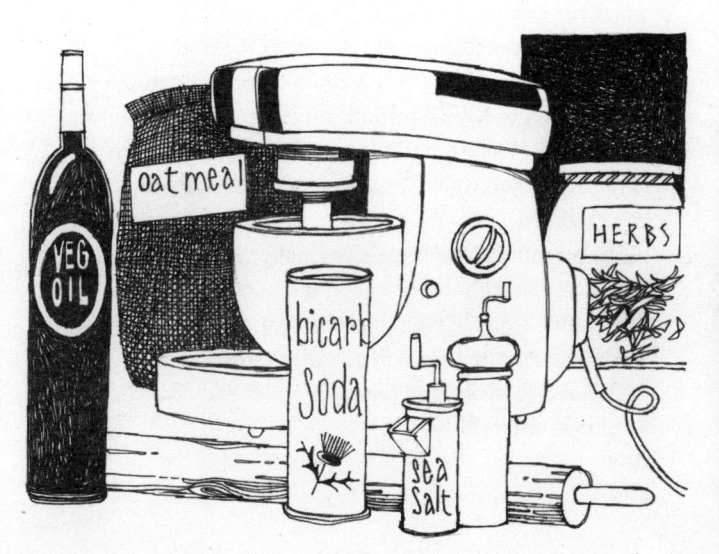

Tattie and spelt crispbreads

A rustic flatbread with taste and crunch to the last bite.

Makes 18 fingers
100g (3½oz) boiled potatoes, riced or mashed (F/AR)
60g (2oz) spelt flour sifted with
1 teaspoon baking powder
2.5g (½ teaspoon) sea salt
10ml (2 teaspoons) oil
Spelt flour to roll

Heat the oven to 180°C (fan 160°C), 350°F, Gas 4. Put the mashed potatoes in a bowl, sift in the flour and baking powder. Add the salt and oil. Fork mix into a pliable dough. Knead smooth on a floured board then cut in two. Roll each thinly to a rectangle 10cm (4in.) wide and prick well. Cut across each rectangle in 5cm (2in.) slices and lay on a non-stick baking tray. Bake for 15 to 20 minutes till crisp. Check after 10 minutes; if colouring quickly reduce oven temperature to 170°C (fan 140°C), 325°F, Gas 4, to ensure a crisp result. Cool on a wire tray and store in an airtight tin.

Blitzed sunflower or pumpkin seeds add crunch, nutrition and taste.

Potato, apple and cinnamon loaf cake

A winner for coffee mornings and fundraising teas. Moistly more-ish to the last crumb.

Makes 2 x 350g (12oz) loaf cakes
45g (1½oz) honey
85g (3oz) soft brown sugar
115g (4oz) margarine
85g (3oz) raw potato, grated (F/AR)
115g (4oz) apple, grated
225g (8oz) self-raising flour
3 teaspoons cinnamon
1 teaspoon baking powder
2 eggs, beaten

Turn on the oven at 180°C (fan 160°C), 350°F, Gas 4, and line two loaf tins. Warm the honey, brown sugar and margarine in a pan. Put the grated potato and apple in a bowl. Sift in the flour, cinnamon and baking powder. Mix together. Pour in the pan contents and mix to a soft dropping consistency with the beaten egg. Divide evenly between the loaf tins and bake for 20 to 25 minutes till firm and the point of a skewer inserted in the middle comes out clean. Cool in the tins, wrap in foil and store in an airtight container. Keep for up to a week in a cool place. Freeze for up to two months.

Fruity tattie buns

During the war ingredients were scarce. Adding mashed potato to baking stretched meagre rations.

Makes 8 muffin cakes
30g (1oz) margarine
30g (1oz) caster sugar
115g (4oz) plain mashed potato (F/AR)
30g (1oz) chunky marmalade or apricot jam
2 teaspoons baking powder
85g (3oz) self-raising flour
1 egg beaten with milk to mix
30g (1oz) chopped dried apricot
Caster or icing sugar to finish

Turn on the oven at 180°C (fan 160°C), 350°F, Gas 4. Line eight muffin tins with paper cases. Cream the margarine and sugar till pale, beat in the mashed potato and marmalade or jam. Sift in the flour and baking powder. Mix to a soft dropping consistency with the egg and milk. Fold in the dried apricot and divide evenly between the muffin cases. Bake for 12 to 15 minutes till risen and firm and the point of a skewer inserted in the middle comes out clean. Cool on a wire rack. Dust with icing or caster sugar and enjoy freshly baked.

Lefse (Norwegian potato pancakes)

My Norwegian friend Espen's favourite soft flatbread, which he enjoys warm rolled with butter, cinnamon and sugar. Some fill lefse with jam, berries or peanut butter! What will you enjoy in yours?

Makes 12 small lefse (pancakes)

Step 1
225g (8oz) mashed potato (F/AR)
15g (½oz) melted butter
½ teaspoon salt
15ml (1 tablespoon) double cream
Mix together. Keep in the fridge overnight.

Step 2
115g (4oz) self-raising flour
Flour to dust
Brown rice flour (optional)

Put the potato mix in a bowl. Break into fine crumbs with a fork, then work in the flour, finally kneading to form a smooth slightly sticky dough. Flour work surface well (I find rice flour less sticky). Turn out the dough, divide into 12 equal pieces, rolling each into a ball. Roll each ball into a thin circle. Heat a thick-bottomed frying pan on medium. The heat is correct when a bead of water dropped on the surface sizzles and evaporates. Bake one pancake at a time. Roll the next while the previous one is cooking. In less than a minute the underside will be browning, turn, bake, then fold in a clean tea towel on a plate to keep warm. Repeat. (I found it difficult to start but soon got into the rhythm.) Serve warm, freshly baked. Store in a sealed bag or box in the fridge for up to a week. Interleaf with baking parchment, seal in a bag or container and freeze for up to six weeks.

Re-heat lefse by running a clean wet hand over the surface to dampen. Heat in a warm frying pan, oven or under the grill. Norwegian lefse bakers use a grooved rolling pin.

Canadian potato candy

Orcadian Margaret Rendall gave me this recipe from Canada, where she lived for many years.

Makes 40 walnut-size candies
60g (2oz) plain mashed potato (F/AR)
15g (½oz) butter
1 teaspoon vanilla or almond essence
225g (8oz) icing sugar – approximately

Finish with:
Walnut or almond halves
Chocolate vermicelli
Cocoa powder
Melted dark chocolate

Mix the mashed potato and butter and beat in the essence and sifted icing sugar. The mixture will be fluid but stiffens to a fondant consistency. Wear food gloves to knead smooth. Roll teaspoon-size pieces into balls. Lay on a plate. Sandwich between two nut halves, roll in cocoa powder or chocolate vermicelli.

To dip in melted chocolate, chill to firm. Use a cocktail stick to dip in chocolate. Before the chocolate sets, coat with chopped nuts or coconut. Set on a tray lined with non-stick paper. Keep in the fridge for up to a week. Arrange a selection in fancy cellophane bags or boxes as a gift.

Misread macaroon bar

Scottish Women's Institute enthusiast Iris McIntosh found a recipe for potato macaroons which I misread. This is the outcome.

Makes 1 slab approximately 20cm x 25cm (8in. x 10in.)
115g (4oz) desiccated coconut, toasted under a medium grill
100g (3½oz) mashed potato (F/AR)
1 teaspoon vanilla essence
1 knob of butter
450g (1lb) icing sugar
150g (3½oz) dark cooking chocolate

Put the potato into a bowl and beat in the icing sugar to make a stiff fondant-like paste. Stir in the coconut. Roll out the paste to approximately 20cm x 25cm (8in. x 10in.), lay into a non-stick tray. Set in a cool place. Melt chocolate, spread over the slab, set, then cut into fingers. Do not chill in the fridge. The chocolate becomes brittle and breaks off the coconut interior.

Keeps for up to a week in the fridge.

Chocolate tattie truffles

My first attempt would have cured any chocoholic. I persevered!

Makes 14
75g (2½oz) cold mashed potato (F/AR)
5g (1 teaspoon) melted butter
½ teaspoon vanilla essence
15ml (1 tablespoon) runny honey, maple or agave syrup
5g (1 teaspoon) icing sugar
15g (½oz) cocoa powder

To coat:
Finely chopped hazelnuts, walnuts or pistachios
Shredded coconut
Cocoa powder
or
150g (3½oz) dark or milk chocolate

Put the truffle ingredients in a bowl and fork to a stiff smooth paste. Wear food gloves for the next step. Put topping ingredients on separate flat plates. Roll teaspoons of mix into balls, then in toppings to coat. Lay on a flat plate. Set in the fridge. Keep chilled in a sealed container for up to 5 days.

To coat truffles in chocolate, freeze for 10 to 15 minutes. Cover a flat plate with non-stick baking paper.

Using a double boiler or microwave, 75 per cent melt the chocolate, remove from the heat and beat to a coating consistency. Spear each truffle with a cocktail stick, dip into the chocolate then lay on the non-stick paper. Chill to set. Leftover chocolate if not overheated may be stored and reused.

Flavours to try

Dark chocolate ginger – 15g (½oz) chopped crystallised ginger

Mocha – 2 teaspoons strong coffee

Chocolate orange – 1 teaspoon grated orange rind and 1 teaspoon orange oil

Free from – omit butter, bind with extra honey or syrup

Gluten-free

Chocolate potato fudge brownie

Mash imparts unique sumptuousness – 'the brownie eating experience'! Creating a 'can't tell it's gluten-free' cake is difficult. I think this one fits the bill, or should I say plate!

Makes a cake 18 x 30cm (7 x 12in)
100ml (3½oz) sunflower oil
85g (3oz) soft brown sugar
85g (3oz) boiled, mashed or riced potato (F/AR)
2 large eggs, beaten
115g (4oz) dark chocolate
150g (5oz) gluten-free self-raising flour
1 teaspoon vanilla essence
30g (1oz) chopped walnuts

Turn on the oven at 180°C (fan 160°C) 350°F, Gas 4. Oil and line a non-stick baking tin. Beat the eggs, oil, sugar and potatoes together. Melt the chocolate on medium power in the microwave or in a bowl over simmering water, stirring till the chocolate is smooth. Beat one tablespoon of the potato mix into the chocolate. Pour the chocolate into the potato mix, sift in the flour, add the vanilla essence and beat till smooth. Stir in the

walnuts. Pour into the baking tin, spread evenly. Bake for
15 minutes or till the cake is firm and springy and the
point of a skewer comes out clean. Cool in the tin.
Spread with topping when cold. Chill for 10 minutes to
set. Cut and enjoy. Store wrapped in foil in a cool place.

Chocolate potato fudge topping

60g (2oz) butter, melted
30g (1oz) cocoa powder
45g (1½oz) boiled mashed or riced potato (F/AR)
30g (1oz) golden syrup
1 teaspoon instant coffee powder
60g (2oz) icing sugar

Beat the ingredients to a thick spreading consistency. Add more icing sugar to thicken if needed.

Mashed tattie gluten-free dropped scones

An afternoon tea party was an opportunity to experiment, normal versus gluten-free with added mash. Guests voted for the mash! The scones remained moist the following day.

Makes 6 to 8 dropped scones

115g (4oz) gluten-free self-raising flour
60g (2oz) plain boiled mashed potato
1 teaspoon gluten-free baking powder
1 egg, beaten
30g (1oz) golden syrup or honey
100ml (3fl oz) milk or dairy-free coconut milk

Heat a girdle or thick-bottomed frying pan on medium heat. Sift the flour and baking powder into a bowl. Add the potato, egg and syrup or honey. Mix with the milk to a thick smooth batter. Use a balloon whisk for lump-free lightness. Test the heat of the girdle with a dust of flour. The temperature is right if it turns golden; reduce the heat if it burns. Rub with oil. Bake tablespoons of batter till bubbles rise and burst. Flip over with a palette knife or fish slice. Tap gently to release trapped air to ensure an even bake. Cool on a wire rack wrapped in a clean tea towel and eat fresh. Indulgence is to drop dark chocolate chips onto the soft uncooked scone surface as it bubbles, flip over to melt and bake. A messy eat but worth it!

Mabel Thomson's tattie wine

Orcadian Richard Shearer of the well-known Kirkwall family firm William Shearer's remembers earlier years when a glass or two of Mabel Thomson's potent tattie wine was a great lubricant at parties. Asked for the recipe and tasting notes, he replied: 'Here is the Tattie Wine recipe (hic!) as promised.'

---

6 medium-size old tatties, washed, peeled and sliced (F/AR/W)
2 lemons and 2 oranges, washed, peeled and sliced
1.3kg (3lb) sugar
450g (1lb) raisins
4.55 litres (1 gallon) water
30g (1oz) brewer's yeast

Place the sliced tatties, lemon and orange in a pot with the raisins and sugar. Pour over boiling water and stir until the sugar is dissolved. When cool but not cold add the yeast. Cover with a tea towel and keep at room temperature. Stir daily for 10 days. Strain and pour into clean sterilised bottles with a tight cap. Leave to cool and store in a cool dark place for 6 to 12 months.

'I will taste in the next few days.'